A PRACTICAL GUIDE TO

GROWING
YOUR OWN
PLANTS

A PRACTICAL GUIDE TO

GROWING YOUR OWN PLANTS

‖ •PARRAGON• ‖

Introduction

With varied planting garden beds and borders can be awash with colour from spring to the onset of winter. Much colour is brought to the garden in spring by flowering bedding plants such as double daisies and wallflowers, which are planted in autumn, along with bulbs like tulips and hyacinths. These are removed once they have ceased flowering and summer-flowering bedding plants put in their place. Herbaceous perennials, however, can be left in one position for three to five years before being lifted, divided and then replanted. Hardy annuals, which are sown in their flowering positions in late spring or early summer, can be used to create beautiful displays later in the same season.

Many plants, like the Mediterranean native *Antirrhinum*, which are grown as hardy perennials in warm countries may be raised as half-hardy annuals in temperate regions. Likewise, plants like sweet williams and daisies, which are perennials in their native countries are invariably grown as biennials in cooler regions.

Some plants which create colourful displays in borders have a tuberous nature. Dahlias, which are available in a vast range of colours, sizes and shapes, are the best known. Most are increased by cuttings or division of the tubers, but the bedding types, with their low-growing nature, are raised from seeds.

The first part of this book looks at the different ways popular plants can be propagated. It gives tips on sowing seeds, both indoors or in a garden and explains how seedlings can be successfully grown and transplanted. Techniques for taking cuttings from stems or leaves are explained in depth.

© Marshall Cavendish 1995

Some of this material has previously appeared in the Marshall Cavendish partwork **My Garden**.

CLB 4383

This edition published 1995 by Parragon Book Services Ltd Unit 13-17 Avonbridge Trading Estate, Atlantic Road Avonmouth, Bristol BS11 9QD.

ISBN 1-85813-827-2
Printed in Hong Kong

Contents

Techniques for Sowing Seeds Outdoors *page 6*

Sowing Seeds Indoors
page 10

Looking After Seedlings
page 16

Transplanting Seedlings
page 21

Taking Stem Cuttings
page 26

Propagating Plants by Layering
page 30

Techniques of Root Propagation
page 34

Making Use of a Greenhouse
page 40

Chrysanthemums
page 44

Dazzling Dahlias
page 50

Glorious Sweet Peas
page 54

Poppies
page 58

Geraniums For Borders
page 64

Delphiniums
page 70

Radiant Sunflowers
page 74

The Fragrant Garden
page 78

Wild Flowers In The Garden
page 84

Budget Gardens
page 90

Index *page 94*

Techniques for Sowing Seeds Outdoors

Raising plants from seeds is an inexpensive way to acquire plants for your garden and sowing seeds outdoors is surprisingly easy once you know how.

A vibrant display of Sweet Williams (Dianthus barbatus) can be grown from seed (left) at a fraction of the price of bedding plants. As this is a biennial, sow the seeds first in a nursery bed and allow the seedlings to develop into strong plants before moving them to their final flowering position. Sweet Williams thrive best in an open position and well-drained soil.

BIENNIALS

Name	Flowering	Planting spacings
Common daisy (Bellis perennis)	Mid spring to mid autumn	13-15cm/5-6in
Canterbury bell (Campanula medium)	Early to mid summer	25-30cm/10-12in
Siberian wallflower (Cheiranthus × allionii)	Late spring to mid summer	25-30cm/10-12in
Sweet William (Dianthus barbatus)	Early to mid summer	20-25cm/8-10in
Foxglove (Digitalis purpurea)	Early to late summer	30-45cm/12-18in
Honesty (Lunaria annua)	Mid spring to early summer	25-30cm/10-12in
Forget-me-not (Myosotis)	Late spring to early summer	15-20cm/6-8in

Whatever their size and shape, seeds need moisture, warmth and air to encourage germination. The majority germinate in darkness, while a few require light. They are therefore scattered on top of the soil or compost rather than being slightly buried.

Moisture is needed to soften the seed's coat and chemically activate the process of growth, while air is required to enable respiration in the roots and developing shoots.

Warmth controls when, and at what rate, the process of germination takes place. As long as the soil or compost is moist, but not waterlogged, and has an open texture to enable air to circulate, the only variable in the process of germination is the temperature.

Germination

The warmth needed to encourage seeds to germinate differs from one type of plant to another. Seeds sown in greenhouses can, of course, be given optimum temperatures to

HARDY ANNUALS

Name	Flowering	Sowing depth	Thin to
Love-lies-bleeding (Amaranthus caudatus)	Mid summer to mid autumn	3mm/½in	30-38cm/12-15in
Pot marigold (Calendula officinalis)	Early summer onwards	12mm/½in	25-30cm/10-12in
Cornflower (Centaurea cyanus)	Early summer to early autumn	12mm/½in	23-38cm/9-15in
Chrysanthemum carinatum (syn. C. tricolor)	Early summer to early autumn	6mm/¼in	15-23cm/6-9in
Clarkia elegans	Mid summer to early autumn	6mm/¼in	25-30cm/10-12in
Clarkia pulchella	Mid summer to early autumn	6mm/¼in	25-30cm/10-12in
Convolvulus tricolor (syn. C. minor)	Mid summer to early autumn	12mm/½in	23-30cm/9-12in
Larkspur Delphinium consolida (syn. Consolida ajacis)	Early to late summer	6mm/¼in	15cm-23cm/6-9in
Californian poppy (Eschscholzia californica)	Early summer onwards	6mm/¼in	23-30cm/9-12in
Gypsophila elegans	Early summer to early autumn	6mm/¼in	23-30cm/9-12in
Sunflower (Helianthus annuus)	Mid summer to early autumn	12mm/½in	30-45cm/12-18in
Candytuft (Iberis umbellata)	Early summer to early autumn	6mm/¼in	23cm/9in
Sweet pea (Lathyrus odoratus)	Early summer to early autumn	12mm/½in	23-30cm/9-12in
Poached egg plant (Limnanthus douglasii)	Early to late summer	3mm/⅛in	10cm/4in
Scarlet flax (Linum grandiflorum)	Early to late summer	6mm/¼in	30-38cm/12-15in
Virginian stock (Malcolmia maritima)	Summer (repeat sowings necessary)	6mm/¼in	15cm/6in
Night-scented stock (Matthiola bicornis)	Mid to late summer	6mm/¼in	23cm/9in
Love-in-a-mist (Nigella damascena)	Early to late summer	6mm/¼in	15-23cm/6-9in
Field poppy (Papaver rhoeas)	Early to late summer	6mm/¼in	25-30cm/10-12in
Mignonette (Reseda odorata)	Early summer to mid autumn	3mm/⅛in	23-30cm/9-12in
Black-eyed Susan (Rudbeckia hirta)	Late summer onwards	6mm/¼in	30-38cm/12-15in

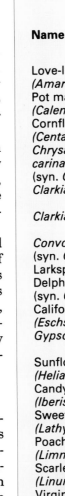

Derek Gould

Hardy annuals such as scarlet flax (Linum grandiflorum 'Rubrum', left) are resilient plants which can simply be sown outdoors where you want them to flower. If they are to form part of a larger bed, make sure you take varying colour combinations into account before sowing.

Encourage sweet pea seeds (right) to germinate rapidly by nicking them lightly with a knife before planting. This helps the hard seed coat to break down.

Harry Smith Collection

7

HARDY HERBACEOUS PERENNIALS

Name	Flowering	Sowing depth	Transplant to
Yarrow (Achillea filipendula)	Mid summer to early autumn	6mm/¼in	38-45cm/15-18in
Yarrow (Achillea millefolium)	Early summer to early autumn	6mm/¼in	30-38cm/12-15in
Anchusa azurea (syn. A. italica)	Early to late summer	12mm/½in	30-38cm/12-15in
Cupid's dart (Catananche caerulea)	Early to mid summer	6mm/¼in	30-38cm/12-15in
Shasta daisy (Chrysanthemum maximum)	Early to late summer	6mm/¼in	30-45cm/12-18in
Coreopsis grandiflora	Early to late summer	6mm/¼in	30cm/12in
Delphinium	Early to mid summer	6mm/¼in	45-60cm/1½-2ft
Globe thistle (Echinops ritro)	Mid to late summer	12mm/½in	45-60cm/18-24in
Blanket flower Gaillardia aristata (syn. G. grandiflora)	Early summer to mid autumn	6mm/¼in	38-45cm/15-18in
Avens (Geum chiloense)	Early summer to early autumn	3mm/⅛in	30-38cm/12-15in
Baby's breath (Gypsophila paniculata)	Early to late summer	6mm/¼in	45-75cm/1½-2½ft
Sweet rocket (Hesperis matronalis)	Early summer	6mm/¼in	38cm/15in
Oriental poppy (Papaver orientale)	Late spring to early summer	6mm/¼in	45-60cm/1½-2ft

encourage germination. Outdoors, this is dictated by the weather and especially by the area in which you live.

Spring is the traditional time of year for sowing seeds because the rising temperatures make germination possible. The range of ornamental plants for sowing outdoors is extremely wide and includes annuals, biennials, herbaceous perennials, trees and, of course, shrubs.

Annuals

Some annuals are half-hardy and must be raised under glass early in the year, ready for planting outdoors as soon as the risk of frost has passed. Hardy annuals have a tougher image and can be sown outdoors in the positions where they are to flower. Most are sown in spring.

Preparation for sowing hardy annuals should begin in the autumn of the previous year, when the soil is dug to a depth of about 25cm/10in (a spade's blade). Well-rotted manure and decayed garden compost can be dug into the soil at this stage, but remember annuals flower best in soil that is not too rich.

Winter weather breaks down large lumps of soil and by spring creates a fine tilth. In early spring, rake the ground level, further breaking down the soil. Firm light soils by systematically treading over them, but take care not to compact them too much.

Small and narrow flower beds at the side of paths can be sown without too much preparation. But large borders need to be carefully planned on paper first, taking into account the differing heights and colour combinations.

After raking and treading the surface, use a thin line of sand to mark out the areas for each type. Alternatively, mark the areas by using a stick to draw shallow lines.

A garden-line and the corner of a hoe or rake can be used to create drills in which seeds can be sown. Sow seeds thinly and evenly and use the back of a rake to cover them. Alternatively, shuffle along the

The hardy herbaceous perennial blanket flower (Gaillardia aristata) will provide a profusion of brilliant yellow blooms (above) for several years, if grown initially from seed in a nursery bed.

When preparing the soil in spring for sowing, first mark out the positions of the different plants you intend to sow with a thin line of sand (right). Then form drills with the side of a hoe. When the seeds are sown, use the back of a rake (inset) to cover them with soil to the required depth.

drill, with your feet on either side of it, gently pushing soil over the seeds.

If you need to lightly rake the surface at this stage, do this in the same direction as the drills. Raking across them may disturb and scatter seeds in the wrong places.

Place brushwood-type sticks over the area to prevent birds and cats scratching the seed. Alternatively, use black cotton stretched between canes inserted at the edges of the border. Extra protection can be given by threading pieces of tin-foil along the cotton.

During dry spells, keep the border moist. After germination, remove the sticks and, when large enough to handle, thin out the seedlings to the distances in the Hardy Annual table on page 1169.

Most of the plants in this table are true hardy annuals but some, such as Black-eyed Susan (*Rudbeckia hirta*), are short-lived perennials which are normally cultivated as hardy annuals.

Biennials

These are plants that are usually sown in shallow drills, about 30-38cm/12-15in apart, in a nursery bed in early summer for flowering during the following year.

During the first few months they germinate and develop into strong plants. Transfer them to their flowering positions in late summer or early autumn.

Many plants naturally have a biennial nature, but others although normally perennial are treated as biennials.

Herbaceous perennials

These are plants that live for several years, dying down to soil level in autumn and sending up fresh shoots the following spring.

They are raised by sowing seeds thinly in shallow drills in a nursery bed in late spring and early summer. The sowing depths are indicated in the Hardy Herbaceous Perennial table on page 1170.

After germination, thin the seedlings slightly so that they are not congested, and in late summer or autumn plant them into their flowering position. The spacings are also indicated in the table. These distances may need to be adjusted according to the height and vigour of a particular variety.

Trees and shrubs

Seeds of trees and shrubs are increasingly offered in seed catalogues and, although it takes many years for a reasonably-sized tree to be raised in this way, to do so always creates a lasting sense of personal achievement.

Seeds of some trees and shrubs are large, with thick coats that reduce the speed of germination. Therefore, it is often necessary to soften or remove part of the seed coat, or to submit them to alternating periods of cold and warmth before they are sown.

Some ways of encouraging the rapid germination of seeds are suggested below.

ENCOURAGING SEEDS

Soaking seeds in water helps to leach out chemicals that inhibit germination. Soak for up to three hours in hand-hot water. If the packet advises soaking for longer, change the water periodically. Some seed, such as clianthus, caragana and broom swell when soaked. If this happens, sow immediately – before they have time to dry out.

Seeds such as sweet peas and morning glory have hard seed coats that benefit from being chipped. Scratch the outer surface with a sharp knife, rub the seeds on fine sand-paper or, with small seeds, prick with a sharp needle.

Some perennials, such as a number of trees, shrubs and many alpines, need a cold period to break their dormancy. This used to be done by putting the seeds between layers of sand and leaving them outside for the winter. Today it is easier to use a refrigerator.

Sow the seeds on several layers of moist kitchen paper placed in a small plastic container with a close-fitting lid. Keep them at room temperature for about three days then place in the refrigerator for several weeks. Check periodically to make sure the kitchen paper has not dried out. Then remove the seeds and sow them in compost.

BRIGHT IDEAS

Eric Crichton

Collections/Patrick Johns

Harry Smith Collection

Sowing Seeds Indoors

Growing from seed is immensely rewarding. Not only is it the cheapest way to fill your garden with masses of blooms, but it is also easy to do.

Growing plants from seed is not a difficult business and it is enormously satisfying to bring on a plant from seed right through to flowering.

Buying seed is, of course, cheaper than buying plants, even allowing for a certain outlay on pots and compost. Perennials, trees and shrubs are slow to grow from seed, and it is usually better to buy an established plant. Annual bedding plants and vegetables, on the other hand, are best raised from seed and this can be done with the minimum of space and equipment.

There is no need for a greenhouse or cold frames. A warm, light windowsill will do perfectly well. By following a few simple guidelines you can produce an excellent stock of bedding plants.

Tools of the trade

You will need compost, a few pots and trays and the seed. Apart from compost and seeds, every piece of equipment can be improvised.

Begin by clearing a table or draining board and set out the containers (seed trays or pots) needed for each batch of seed. Shallow (half) pots or plastic seed trays are best for sowing seed. The seedlings are

'pricked out' soon after their first leaves appear so a greater depth of compost would be wasted. The plastic punnets or trays in which you buy your fruit and vegetables from the supermarket are ideal. Yoghurt pots or old plastic

cups will do the job too. With a screwdriver, punch holes in the bottom for drainage. Cut cups down to 6cm/2½in high if you want to be economical with your compost.

Most seed packets contain a generous amount and you will

Fill your garden with masses of summer flowers for a fraction of the cost of ready-grown bedding plants.

Show lupins off to best effect in the middle of a border.

Easy-to-grow sweet peas make wonderful cut flowers.

Begonias, in beds or containers, will flower all summer long.

EASY STEPS TO SOWING SEEDS

1 *Fill the seed tray with compost almost to the top. Compress the compost with another tray.*

2 *Water thoroughly by setting of tray in a bowl of water. L for a few moments.*

6 *Lupin seeds are quite large. Sow two then discard the weaker seedling later.*

7 *Cover seeds with 1.5cm/¹/₂i compost. Water lightly so th seeds are undisturbed.*

not need the entire contents. Sow some of the seed into a small tray or 'half tray' (15 x 20cm/6 x 8in) and save or give away the rest.

Some seeds, such as sweet peas, lupins and pot marigolds are best sown in individual pots, which allows them to grow on with their roots undisturbed right from the start. (Small yoghurt pots are quite big enough to start with.)

There are many brands of seed compost available, and one will work just as well as another. The advantage of these composts is that they are fine-textured and contain no strong nutrients which might upset tiny seedlings. So do not be tempted to make do with stronger potting composts. Invest in a little of the right compost and it will help you to avoid set-backs with your seedlings' growth.

See the light

The seed containers should be filled evenly with compost, including the four corners of trays. Fill them loosely to the top, then take a second container of the same shape and use its base to press down the compost, firming it to a level within 6mm/¼in of the top. If

3 Alternatively, gently pour water over the seed tray (without disturbing the surface too much).

4 Begonia seeds are like specks of dust. A capsule that may come with the seeds helps sow them evenly.

5 Do not cover begonia seeds with compost. Cover with cling film to create humidity for germination.

8 A plastic bottle 'cloche' provides moist conditions for germination. For ventilation, open the bottle top.

9 Sow sweet pea seeds in moistened peat pots. These can be put straight into the ground at planting time.

10 Seal opened seed packets with cling film and store in a cool, dry place until next year.

Ray Duns

you leave the compost level much below that, the sides of the pot will reduce the light which reaches the seedlings. Maximum light and air are vital for healthy seedlings.

It is more practical to water the compost thoroughly at this stage. This avoids the need to water heavily after sowing, which can wash the seeds around on the surface of the compost and undo all your careful, even sowing.

The best method of watering is with a watering can with a good quality, fine metal rose on the end. Plastic roses are often very crude and spluttery, suitable only for garden use; it is worth buying a good rose that will fit your can. Alternatively, lower the pot's base gently into a bowl of water to soak the compost for a few seconds – *before* you sow your seeds. Allow the compost to drain a little before sowing.

Indoors or out?

Before rushing to sow, first check the seed packet for the precise instructions and requirements. For example, some annual flowers can be sown outdoors in situ. Others need to be sown indoors, but not covered with soil, since they require light for germination, for example, begonia.

To sow seed from a packet into the prepared container, shake the seed down to the bottom of the packet before tearing off the tip. This prevents spillage; generally seeds come in a sealed pack within the packet. Then, holding the packet on its side over the container, between thumb and middle finger, gently tap the packet with your index finger to produce a gradual trickle of seed. Move the packet around until the surface of the compost is thinly and evenly covered. Too thickly sown

WATERING

Small seedlings require very little water (except sweet peas), and there is no need to water often. As you grow them on and the plant develops, they will require more water. In the early stages, moistness is all that is necessary.

A cling film covering or home-made cloche helps provide a moist environment.

seed will produce crammed, crowded seedlings that are difficult to separate and pot on. They are also much more likely to go mouldy.

Do not feel you have to use the whole packet of seed. Save some for a later sowing, perhaps, or even for next year. Most seed will keep for 12 months in a cool place in an airtight container, even if it gives a slightly lower percentage of germination. Seal the packet in foil or cling film to help prevent deterioration.

Once the seed is sown it needs to be covered with the required depth of compost. (Check the seed packet details.) You can do this by using a loosely cupped hand as a sieve, shaking it over the pot to allow a thin trickle of compost to escape between your fingers. A very coarse kitchen sieve will do the job nicely too, but fine meshes hold back too much of the compost fibre.

Settling in

Give the containers a final watering to bed in the seed. Using a fine rose, pass the watering can once or twice quickly over the top; just enough to settle the surface. Try to make sure the can is already flowing before you spray it over the compost, to avoid the first, sudden spurts of water. This can splash in the earth and disturb the surface.

Find a warm and (in most cases) dark place to keep the containers until the seeds germinate. Once again, the seed packet will say whether a particular variety needs light and, sometimes, how long the seed will take to germinate. Some can sprout in just a few days, others take up to three weeks. (Some can take months, but these are usually hardy perennials rather than annuals).

Some seeds demand higher temperatures to germinate. In these cases, an airing cupboard provides an even, warm environment for germination, both day and night.

Covering up

To stop the compost drying out and save you the daily task of methodical watering, cover the containers. There are various methods. Glass used to be the traditional way, but, with small pots of seed, a little 'mob cap' made from polythene with an elastic band to hold it in

DON'T FORGET!

WHAT COMPOST?
The right compost is vital for successful seeds. Special seed composts, like John Innes, contain balanced nutrients and the correct texture.

For a modest outlay, this propagation kit (right), available from garden centres and shops, contains seed trays with lids and separate modules for pricking out. This kit allows you to grow 24-96 plants.

PROJECT PROPAGATING SEEDS ON A WINDOWSILL

The most ideal conditions for raising seeds are in a greenhouse or conservatory. This propagator box will give you excellent results from your windowsill. The foil acts as a reflector, so the seedlings receive all round light. This prevents 'legginess' – a common problem.

All you need is a cardboard box, kitchen foil, glue, sticky tape or stapler.

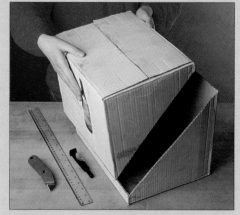

Choose a box which has a base area large enough for one or more seed trays but which can also fit near a light window. Cut the box as shown above.

Cover the inside with kitchen foil, shiny side outwards. Fix into position. Place seed trays in as shown. Remove from windowsill in frosty weather.

Ray Duns

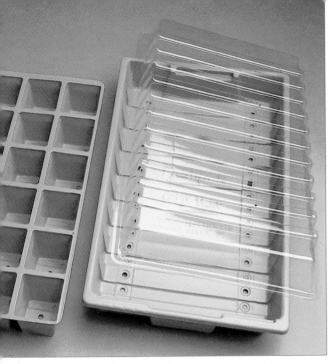

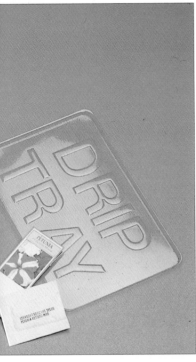

There are several variations of a more complete sowing kit on a smaller scale. This kit (left) contains seed tray, with drip tray and lid, seeds and compost. All you need to add is water and warmth.

Put together your own seed-raising kit for free. Recycle plastic vegetable and fruit packaging trays (below), yoghurt pots and margarine cartons. Don't forget to make some holes for drainage.

place will do just as well. Pierce a couple of holes to stop the air getting stale.

The condensation that builds up on the underside of the polythene drops onto the compost and keeps it moist. It will, however, need to be wiped off or turned over every other day or so. While you are doing this, keep a sharp eye open for the first emerging green shoots.

As an alternative to polythene covers, use very large clear plastic lemonade bottles with their bottoms cut off. These make splendid little 'greenhouses' and the screw-top serves as an excellent ventilator. For seed trays, use sheets of cling film or polythene pierced with a few fine holes for ventilation.

Timing counts

If you are growing annuals from seed without a cold frame, do not be tempted to sow too early. Without a cold frame in which to harden off young plants and accustom them to life outdoors, it is always best to sow at the end of the advised period on the packet. If you sow too soon your plants will be ready to go outside before the weather is warm enough and danger of frost is past.

Windowsills often have inadequate light which makes seedlings 'leggy'. To overcome this, make a propagator (far left) which maximizes the amount of light available. Plants which are grown late, but well, often overtake plants which were sown too early and have suffered setbacks.

The first shoots

Once the seedlings germinate and the shoots appear, uncover the containers and move them to a light windowsill which is also warm. A cold, draughty sill may kill off your seedlings. If this is the case, move them off the window-sill to a warmer position overnight when the temperature drops.

DON'T FORGET!

SHOW A LEG

Q Why do my seedlings often grow long stems in a lop-sided way?

A Seedlings grow towards the light. As soon as seedlings appear, turn the tray regularly so they receive even sunlight.

Modern, draught-proof and double-glazed windows are perfect. Here, the seedlings can continue to develop steadily until the first pair of 'seed leaves' are fully formed.

This is the time to separate the seedlings and prick them out into trays or pots. Whether you use one or the other at this stage is largely a matter of space. Trays allow you to put more plants into a smaller space, but when you come to plant them out there is more chance of disturbing the plants' roots.

One for the pot

Individual pots, however, allow the plants to develop a root system which can be lifted out without any disturbance or setback at planting time. For instance, sweet peas can be planted singly in peat pots. These can be planted straight into the ground, where they break up into the soil. Seedlings in individual pots can also be moved and spaced out individually as they grow on, to give them maximum light for bushier growth.

If you are limited to growing plants on your windowsills, then you might try modular trays. There are many brands available, but the basic idea is the same. A rectangular tray is divided into smaller units. Each plant has its own container, but the plants are held conveniently together. When you want to remove the young plants from the modules, simply press the bottom of the individual pocket to release the rootball.

Looking After Seedlings

Seeds sown indoors in the last two or three weeks should have germinated by now. Here's what to do next.

Photos Horticultural

As soon as your seedlings have produced their first pair of tiny green leaves it is time to give them a bit of space, or 'prick them out'.

Densely sown crops of seedlings are prone to damping off at this stage, so pricking them out while they are still small is very important. With tiny seed-lings, it can be a rather fiddly job, but it is perfectly possible with a little practice.

As a general rule, prick out only the strongest seedlings and discard any that are weak or spindly. However, with mix-tures prick out both strong and weak to ensure a good col-our balance. Lobelia seedlings are tiny and are pricked out in small clusters, so some will in-evitably be at a later stage of development than others.

Seedlings can be pricked out into pots, trays or modules (trays with their own internal divisions). Modules are econ-omical on compost and space and are easy to handle. There

Growing plants from seed is not only immensely satisfying it is also very economical. Once your seeds have germinated you will be rewarded with trays full of densely packed seedlings (above). This is the stage at which you prick them out, to prevent overcrowding.

When the first two leaves appear the seedlings should be transplanted in order to give their root system adequate space to develop. The seedlings (left) have outgrown their tray and are being transplanted into another container where they will have adequate breathing space. The pansy seedlings (right) have been planted in individual containers until they are ready for planting out. Seedlings, like babies, cannot digest strong foods so plant in specially balanced seedling compost.

Andrew Lawson

is also no disturbance to roots when the time comes to plant out, so the plants suffer no disruption to their growth.

Traditional seed trays (containing five rows of eight plants) are fine, but there will be a period, after the roots have been disturbed at planting out time, when growth is temporarily slowed down.

Which pot?

Pots can be used for seedlings, but they must be small (6-7.5cm/2½-3in across). A smaller pot is more economical on both space and compost and seedlings can later be moved to a larger one, if necessary.

To prick out seedlings, first fill your trays, pots or modules with compost, right up to the top. Press the compost down gently to leave space for watering. Make a hole with a pencil or a piece of fine cane. Then, using finger and thumb, take hold of the first seedling by one of its leaves. Use the pencil to gently tease up the root from the compost, then lower it into the prepared hole. Use the pencil again to bring the soil up to the root. When the tray is full, give it a thorough watering with tepid water through a fine rose. Seedlings hate an icy shower! Once the tray has drained, it is ready to go on the window sill.

The temperature needed

Photos Horticultural

Not all seedlings look the same. Some, like these cyclamen (left) are quite developed and already share a family resemblance. They produce 'true' leaves unlike most seedlings whose first pair of leaves bears no resemblance to their final form.

The cyclamen produces a root ball which can easily be replanted while the sweet peas (below) set out a long tap root which must be handled carefully. Make a deep hole and insert the seedling, taking care not to break the root.

DON'T FORGET!

VITAL NEEDS

To ensure that seedlings grow into compact, healthy plants remember to give them:
- maximum light
- maximum ventilation
- an even temperature
- soil that is moist but not saturated

now is not quite so high as it was for germination. Over the next few weeks it needs to be gradually lowered to steady the growth of your little plants. Remember, though, that the temperature should not vary too much. If you are growing your plants on the window sill, lift them away

Peter McHoy

PRICKING OUT SEEDLINGS

When your seed tray begins to look overcrowded, the time has come to give the seedlings a bit of room. The next stage in the process of raising seedlings is known as pricking out. It is a fiddly job because the seedlings are so small but it will pay dividends in the long run. The size of the seedlings depends on the plant. Some, like the begonias pictured below, have tiny seeds and very small seedlings. Cyclamen and sweet pea seedlings are larger and easier to handle. They can be transplanted into modular trays which have individual compartments for each seedling or into individual small pots.

1 *Fill a modular tray with special compost suitable for seedlings and water well.*

2 *Using a pencil, ease out the roots and lift by the leaves using thumb and forefinger.*

3 *Make a hole in the compost with the pencil, insert the seedling and firm in.*

4 *Using the blunt end of the pencil gently firm in the soil around the seedlings.*

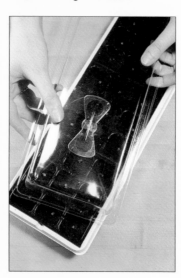

5 *Put a lid on the tray or cover pots with cling film to preserve moisture.*

Marshall Cavendish

OUTDOOR SOWING

Of course, the information on these pages applies only to seed sown indoors, and if the notes on your seed packet tell you to sow directly into the ground where the plants are to flower, you should follow this advice instead. Not all plants are automatically better suited to being nurtured indoors. Poppies, larkspur and pot marigolds will all produce far better plants when sown straight into the soil outdoors.

Photos Horticultural

from the window into the room at night, so they do not get chilled. This is especially important at first, while the seedlings are getting established. Later, they will need to become accustomed to a colder night-time temperature before they go outside. A temperature of about 15-18°C/60-65°F is suitable for most new seedlings, reducing to 10–13°C/50-55°F later on.

While your seedlings are growing on, it is important to maintain as high a level of light as you possibly can. This will prevent the plants from becoming drawn and leggy. It is advisable to turn the trays or pots every few days so that both sides of the plants receive light and develop evenly.

At this stage bedding plants should be bushing out rather

WHAT DOES IT MEAN?

- **Pricking out** – spacing out seedlings in seed trays or pots.
- **Hardening off** – the process of acclimatizing tender and half-hardy seedlings raised indoors or under glass to the harsher conditions which exist out of doors.
- **Growing on** – the stage during which transplanted seedlings establish themselves and grow larger, before they are finally planted out of doors.
- **Damping off** – not a technique, but a fungus that can infect seedlings soon after they have germinated. For this reason, you should use only sterilized compost. Poor drainage and over-watering can also encourage the problem. Remove plastic coverings for a short period each day so that the atmosphere is not too humid. Always wash old pots and trays thoroughly before use, and water seedlings with fresh tap water.

Prevention is better than cure for controlling damping off. Keep tools clean and never use garden soil.

than making one tall shoot. If they are shooting upwards it means either that they are getting insufficient light or that they are too warm, or both. It may be necessary to pinch out the tops to encourage them to bush out.

Hardening off

As the days grow warmer it will be necessary to acclimatize your young plants to conditions out of doors. Hardening off is really just a matter of easing the transition from an 'intensive care' window sill to life in the real world of the flower bed.

Choose a mild, dull day to lift your pots and trays outside for a few hours. The temperature will not be too much of a shock, but they will not be used to the movement of air and it will take time for them to get used to transpiring, or breathing, at a faster rate. If your plants wilt the first time you put them outside, the chances are that they are having difficulty coping with the

A permanent cold frame is often a wooden construction with a glass top. This very professional looking example (right) is located in a sheltered spot by the side of a large greenhouse. The chains attached to the glass top allow the amount of ventilation to be controlled according to the specific requirements of individual plants. Because it is in sections there can be a degree of flexibility – so that some plants can have full ventilation while others are only exposed a little.

Harry Smith

wind and sun. Try again on a balmier day. Eventually, after a few spells outdoors, they will be ready to take direct sun and wind. At this stage they will need more water than before.

Cold frames

The more gently seedlings are hardened off the better, and the easiest place for this is in a cold frame. A cold frame is simple to construct and it will save you all the bother of lifting plants into the garden and back indoors each day. More importantly, a cold frame ensures that your plants are sheltered, receive maximum daylight and develop evenly.

Another advantage is that plants get plenty of ventilation. You can air your young plants constantly in clement

Once the seedlings have been transplanted they have to acclimatize to outside conditions. If you have a cold frame (below) it is easy to control the amount of air your plants receive and at the same time ensure they get maximum daylight. This ensures that your batch of seedlings develop evenly.

Peter McHoy

TAKING CARE

Tiny seedlings are very fragile and some are so small they can be very difficult to handle. Seedlings should be pricked out when the first pair of leaves appear. Always try to lift the seedlings by these leaves. Never attempt to lift a seedling by the stem or roots as these are easily damaged and this may prevent the young plants growing into healthy adults.

Harry Smith

weather and this is a great help in keeping fungal disease at bay.

Having transferred your plants to a cold frame, lift off the cover or prop it open whenever there is a suitably warm and sunny day. It should be open just as much as the plants can stand, to get that vital air through to them. This applies on a wet day just as much as on a dry one, but use a propped lid to let the rain run off and save the seedlings from becoming saturated.

A rain check

Once you have a cold frame you must keep an eye on the weather. When the sun shines,

open the cover quickly so that plants are not roasted. At night, close the frame to protect plants from the chill or, even worse, frost. Once plants are acclimatized to the open air you can leave the cover off at night when the weather is mild.

Planting out

As soon as the risk of frost is past (May or June, depending on where you live), your plants should be planted out into their final positions to give them the maximum growing season. Left in their trays, they will stop growing as they will have used up all the nutrients in the compost.

PROJECT

BUILDING A SIMPLE COLD FRAME

A cold frame need not be large or permanent. It can be made from readily available materials and requires no special skill to assemble.

Site your frame in a warm, sheltered position that receives maximum light. For a frame measuring 1m/3ft 4in square, build up 48 bricks, layer by layer, on a flat surface, following the photographs. Make the joints of each layer overlap the joints of the previous one. There is no need to use mortar between the bricks so the frame can be dismantled easily and moved or stored for the winter.

Once you have built the walls of the frame, place a sheet of rigid clear pvc on top and secure around the edge using more bricks.

To ventilate the frame, remove the cover and place one of the securing bricks diagonally across each corner of the frame walls. Set the cover down again, resting it on the four bricks. Place the remaining four bricks across the corners of the cover, to hold it in place.

For a cheaper alternative to rigid pvc you could try using polythene, or a sheet of glass (in a wooden frame), though this can be risky with children around. Corrugated plastic is strong, but will leave a gap around the sides, even when closed.

1 *Using 48 ordinary household bricks, make a base for your cold frame.*

2 *Place a sheet of rigid clear pvc on top of the wall of bricks.*

3 *You will need another 8 bricks to secure the corners of the pvc.*

4 *To ventilate, simply raise the pvc up one level of the securing bricks.*

Transplanting Seedlings

Whether you grow new plants from seeds or cuttings, they will need transplanting – and if they are to establish well, it pays to know how to do it properly.

Transplanting means moving young plants from one place to another. This includes pricking out young seedlings, potting up rooted cuttings, and moving slightly older seedlings to pots or to the open ground for growing on.

All these jobs involve some degree of stress for the plants. When you dig them up, the fine root hairs that take water into the plant are damaged. Small plants and seedlings contain very limited reserves of water inside them, so any interruption to their water supply will cause a temporary check in growth.

The better the transplanting procedure and environment, the faster new root hairs will be made, and the faster young plants will recover from the shock. Without the right care, they can be slow to establish or, worse still, they may be seriously damaged, prone to diseases or even killed.

Good practice

The real secret of successful transplanting is attention to detail. Good soil preparation and the right before and after care of seedlings and young plants is vital.

Although different groups of plants are propagated at different times, using a wide range of methods, the basic transplanting techniques are the same for all plants.

Check seedlings often to see when they are the right size

When bedding out petunias (right), seedlings should be hardened off outside and then planted out in the garden in spring or early summer, depending on the weather.

Tania Midgley

WHAT YOU NEED

Seed trays and pots – cleaned and ideally rinsed in greenhouse disinfectant before use to kill fungal organisms.

Seed compost – any good brand based on loam, peat or cocopeat but not on garden soil, as it has a poor structure and, if not sterilized, may contain weed seeds, pests and diseases. For best results, use a potting compost with the same base for pricking out.

Plant labels – for labelling young plants and cuttings after potting. Labels often come with a suitable pen or pencil. Slide labels down the side of pots to prevent root damage.

Dibber – short, pointed plastic or cane stick for lifting out seedlings when pricking out. You can use the tip of a pencil.

Trowel – small, narrow, bladed hand trowel for digging up seedlings and transplanting into garden beds.

Spade handle – an old spade handle, cut to 30-45cm/12-18in and pointed at one end, is useful for making the holes for transplanting brassicas. By pushing this into the soil you compact the ground, which produces tighter heads on sprouts and cabbages.

Watering can – buy one with interchangeable heads. Use the fine rose for watering seedlings and young plants.

Polypropylene fleece or old net curtains – for shading seedlings and newly potted plants for 1-2 weeks after potting.

Cloches – for good establishment of outdoor transplants, and for growing on early crops.

Collections/Patrick Johns

Tomato seedlings are pricked out into an individual pot (left) after seed has been sown in a seed tray. An old pen can make a useful dibber.

Calabrese seedlings (below) should be pricked out from their initial seed tray into another tray of the same seed compost. Transplant them when they have their first pair of true leaves, spacing them 5-8cm/2-3in apart. Grow them on in a light position at 10-16°C/50-61°F.

for pricking out. The best time is while they are small, after the cotyledons (seed leaves) have unfolded and the first true leaf has opened out.

The day before you intend to prick out, water the seedlings thoroughly. This way, the seedlings will be fully primed with water, and the compost will be soft and crumbly so the roots will lift easily out without risk of breaking.

Seedlings bought from shops, garden centres or by mail order have often been grown in tiny pots (below). Soak their compost well before planting them in larger pots.

Pricking out

Prepare a clean seed tray or pots, filled with the same sort of seed compost you used to sow the seed. Level the surface and firm the compost by tapping it down lightly. Do not water it yet.

Give the tray of seedlings a sharp tap on a flat surface to loosen them. To prick out, use a dibber or the tip of a pencil to lift the seedlings carefully out of the compost.

Hold seedlings gently, picking up one of the seed leaves between thumb and forefinger.

Photos Horticultural

Eric Crichton

ANNUAL FLOWERS AND BEDDING PLANTS

- Sow seed very thinly and in good light, or seedlings will be drawn up, leggy and rather difficult to prick out.
- Choose the stockiest seedlings for pricking out – leggy ones fall easy prey to fungal diseases.
- When pricking out mixed colour varieties of bedding plants, always select a mixture of large and small seedlings, and a range of leaf shades. By choosing those that look all exactly the same, the odds are that they will all turn out to have flowers of the same colour.
- To get nice bushy plants or if handling very thickly sown seedlings, prick out small clumps instead of individual seedlings.
- Nowadays many seed firms supply seedlings grown as 'plugs' – these have been grown in very tiny containers from which they are removed before posting. What you get is a small young plant with a solid plug of root; these should be soaked in water for 10 minutes if dry, planted in pots or trays immediately and watered in.

Harry Smith Collection

Do not hold the stem, as the plant will not survive if you damage this.

Use the dibber to make a hole in the new compost. You can either plant the seedling to its original depth or drop the roots and stem into a deeper hole, so the seed leaves are just above the surface of the compost. Use the dibber to gently firm the compost around the roots.

If you have a large area to fill with bedding plants (right), plan in advance which species are to go where. Mark off your design with a trickle of sand. Position the young plants on the ground at the correct spacing (below) to make sure that you have enough plants.

If pricking out into a tray (as you do with bedding plants, for instance), space the seedlings about 2.5cm/1in apart. If you only want a few seedlings of, say, houseplants, you need only prick out 10 or so into a 12.5cm/5in half pot. If pricking out large seedlings, such as marrow or sweetcorn, it is best to put each one into a small individual pot.

Watering

After pricking out, water in immediately. Large seedlings can be watered using a watering can with a fine rose. Small seedlings are best watered by standing their tray in a shallow dish of tepid water, until the water soaks through to the surface. You can tell when this happens as the compost turns a darker colour. The idea is to settle the compost around the roots, as well as to moisten it

Andrew Lawson

When you are happy with the arrangement of plants, dig a hole with a trowel (above) to the correct depth. Keep as much compost as possible around the roots and put the plant in carefully.

Firm the soil around the roots of the young plants to get rid of air pockets. Water them in thoroughly (below) until the soil is puddled. Do not let the soil dry out but be careful not to overwater.

thoroughly. Allow surplus water to drain away before standing pots in saucers.

It is not only rooted cuttings that are potted up. Very often you will want to pot up large seedlings (of houseplants perhaps) that have been pricked out into trays or pots and have now filled up all the space.

Potting up

The timing of potting up is much less critical than it is for pricking out. Young plants can be kept in trays or pots for several weeks after rooting, but you must feed them after four to six weeks.

Prepare young plants for transplanting by watering them with half strength liquid feed one or two days beforehand. Before potting up, make sure you have enough clean pots and potting compost.

Loosen the young plants by tapping their pot or tray sharply on a flat surface, and lift individual plants out with your fingers.

Choose pots of a size that take the plant roots easily with space to spare. Traditionally, 9cm/3½in pots are used for the first potting.

Place a little compost in the bottom of the pot, then hold the plant in position with its

roots well spread out while you trickle more compost round them. When the pot is full, check to see the plant is upright and in the centre of the pot, then tap the pot to consolidate the compost.

After potting, water plants in by standing the pots in 5-8cm/2-3in of water, or use a small watering can.

Transplanting outside

Some plants are transplanted straight from seed trays into open ground to save the time and/or cost of pricking them out into compost first. This happens with vegetables and other relatively cheap plants.

They can also be sown into open ground and then transplanted – useful if you have no covered propagating area.

In both cases, prepare seedlings for transplanting by watering well the day before. Prepare the ground where the seedlings are to be transplanted by forking in plenty of well rotted organic matter (unless this has already been done the previous autumn).

If you only have a small

Peter McHoy

PERENNIAL FLOWERS

Sow in midwinter under heated glass to flower the same year (though not all perennials will do so), or in early summer in the open to flower the following year. If sowing early, prick seedlings out into trays or individual pots and transplant to final positions in late spring. If sowing in early summer, sow in an outdoor seedbed, transplant in late summer to rows 30cm/12in apart, then again to their final positions in mid autumn or in the following spring.

BIENNIAL FLOWERS

Sow Canterbury bells, wallflowers and plants that are treated as biennials, such as polyanthus, in rows in the vegetable garden in early summer. Thin them and transplant to final positions in early autumn.

ROSES, TREES AND SHRUBS

Root softwood cuttings in pots in midsummer, hardwood cuttings in the open or in a cold frame in mid to late autumn. You can sow seed in late autumn; it needs cold to germinate and some species take two winters to come up.

Transplant hardwood cuttings when they are well rooted and after new top growth has been made. Lift them with a fork in spring, 18 months after planting. Shorten long stems to improve shape, and 'line out' in rows in a spare patch or in the vegetable garden for a year before planting in their final positions.

Pot softwood cuttings up in mid autumn or early spring when the new plants are well rooted.

Pot seedlings when they are large enough to handle. Pot them individually in 12.5cm/5in pots and transplant them to their final positions when big enough.

Gillian Beckett

amount or are using expensive peat or cocopeat, rake it into the soil surface.

Next spread a base fertilizer dressing of Growmore or Blood, Fish and Bone. Rake it in, levelling the soil and removing large stones as you go.

Use a hand trowel to dig up the seedlings and to make holes for re-planting them in their final positions. Check seed catalogues for spacing of individual vegetables; bedding plants are normally planted about 15-20cm/6-8in apart.

Place the plant into the hole with its roots well spread out, and trowel loose soil around it to fill in the hole.

Seedlings that have not been previously pricked out should be planted deeply, so their seed leaves lie just above the level of the soil. Young plants that have already been pricked out should be transplanted to the same depth they were growing in their pots or trays.

After transplanting, water young plants in well. Use a watering can or a trickling hosepipe to 'puddle' the soil round the roots.

Aftercare

After transplanting, seedlings and young plants should go into 'intensive care' for a week or two. While making new roots, they need partial shade, humidity and light watering.

Seedlings in a greenhouse or cold frame are best covered loosely with an old net curtain or thin cotton sheeting.

In the garden, new trans- plants are best protected by draping polypropylene fleece (a very fine white woven plastic fabric) over them. This also protects them from birds, wind and cold. Failing that, a cloche, or two layers of wire netting with a single thickness of newspaper sandwiched between is the answer.

Check new transplants often, and water whenever the soil looks like starting to dry out. Under-watering is safer than over-watering – too much water will make the roots rot.

Collections/Patrick Johns

A pot of lilac cuttings (above) planted in a mixture of peat and sand. With lilac you should take heel cuttings, tearing the cutting off the plant with a piece of older wood at the base. Pull off the lower leaves and insert the bottom half of the 10-15cm/4-6in cutting in a pot. Cuttings should be taken in mid to late summer. They will root best in a heated propagator, or you can put pots in a cold frame with the lights closed. Keep the atmosphere moist. Pot up rooted cuttings and grow them on in a cold frame. Plant them in a nursery bed in spring. In two to three years they can be transplanted to their final positions.

Trees and shrubs can be propagated from hardwood cuttings (left). These often have a heel attached. Take long cuttings of 15-38cm/6-15in between mid autumn and early spring. Trim each one below a leaf node. In well-drained, fertile soil, dig a slit trench. Put 2.5cm/1in of coarse sand in the bottom. Drop in cuttings to about half their length and firm the soil. They will take up to a year to root and can then be transplanted to their final site.

Taking Stem Cuttings

Taking cuttings is the most cost-effective way of increasing your stock of garden plants – and it's so simple, too. Just follow these basic guidelines.

Marshall Cavendish

Have you ever seen a plant in a friend's garden you would love to have and don't know where to find? Have you a particularly successful specimen in your own garden that you would like more of? In fact, it is really quite easy to make more of them – all you need to do is learn the simple art of taking cuttings.

When you take a stem cutting you remove a stem from a plant and encourage it to form roots to support itself as a new and separate plant.

There is nothing difficult about stem cuttings as the basic operation is really very straightforward. What you do need to remember is that there are right and wrong times to take a cutting, depending on the plant. A cutting taken at the best time will always stand a much greater chance of succeeding.

How and when

Some plants will root in a jar of water or straight into the ground. Others need more controlled conditions. Some cuttings need to be taken when the plant is in full leaf and growth, and need careful attention to tide them over that critical period before the formation of new roots. Others can be taken when the plant is dormant, making the process less stressful for the cutting. Different plants respond differently to different methods.

One thing about stem cuttings is certain: they are a very cheap way of obtaining new plants. Often from the purchase of a single plant you can make dozens of cuttings several times a season. Young

When you are in a friend's garden and you see a plant you would like to have in your own garden ask if you can take a stem cutting (above) you can guarantee that if it is successful it will look exactly like its parent plant. As this chart (right) shows there are a few basic seasons for taking cuttings. Softwood cuttings taken in spring are ideal for delphinimums chrysanthemums and dahlias. Take semi-ripe cuttings in late summer with a 'heel' of older wood.

plants from cuttings can make an interesting and lucrative stall at a bazaar – you will find yoghurt cartons are usually quite acceptable as plant pots.

Plant clones

Unlike a plant grown from seed, a cutting has the advantage of being identical to its parent plant. So if you take a liking to a plant variety in a friend's garden, a cutting will give you the same specimen. Plants produced in this way are said to be of the same clone, which simply means that they all stem from identical genetic material.

This is especially useful where uniformity is needed in the garden. For instance, a yew or cypress hedge made from cuttings from one particular plant will give you a hedge of even greenness and density of habit. Hedges from seed-grown plants will always show individual colour and density variation; growth rates will vary, too.

When it comes to cuttings, as with so much else, you get the best from the best. Good strong healthy shoots always produce better plants and root more easily. Of course, you will not want to disfigure a favourite plant or spoil its shape, but spare a little of it for cuttings as it will pay off later. It is no surprise that in nurseries cuttings are taken from carefully grown stock plants trained to produce ideal cutting material even if they have a poor shape.

Collecting cuttings

When a plant is in leaf and growing strongly, it is best to take cuttings when it is as full of sap as possible – so avoid midday or very hot weather. The day after a heavy rain storm is ideal, as the plants will have had a good long drink. Early morning is another good time, before the heat of the day reduces the moisture level within the leaves.

If you are collecting cuttings from the garden, cut a slightly

SHORT CUTS

EASY OPTIONS

Some plants are very easy to grow from cuttings. Geraniums or fuchsias will root at almost any time during the growing season. Busy Lizzies and willow will root in a jar of water on a window sill. Roses are worth trying as hardwood cuttings, any time between late summer and the middle of winter.

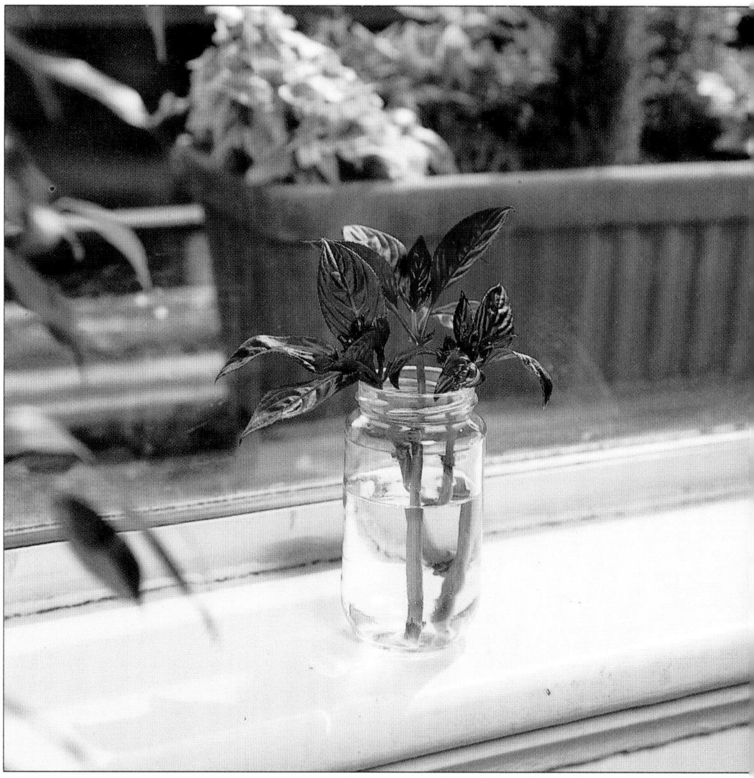

Marshall Cavendish

GARDEN NOTES

HEEL CUTTINGS

Semi-ripe cuttings are often taken with a heel of older wood attached. By pulling rather than cutting off a side shoot, a little of the older wood on the main stem comes away with the cutting. Using a very sharp knife, trim it clean of any damaged tissue (without removing the heel), before rooting it.

Some plants such as the buzy Lizzie (above) are so keen to propagate that they need practically no encouragement. All you have to do is cut off a piece, strip off the bottom leaves and stick it in a jar of water.

To propagate thuja take semi-ripe cuttings with a heel. Instead of cutting through the stem pull off a side shoot taking a little old wood with you (below).

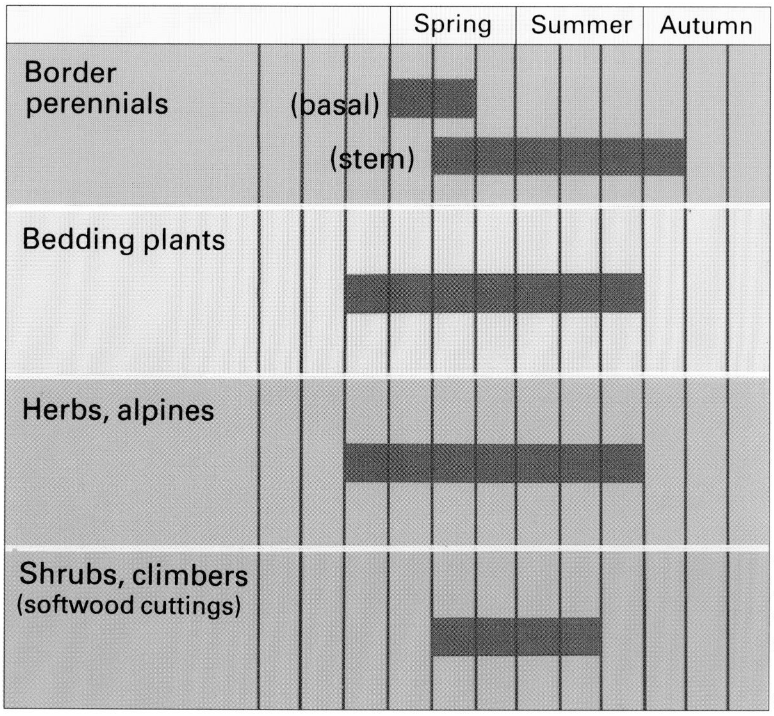

Spring
Summer
Autumn
Border perennials
(basal)
(stem)
Bedding plants
Herbs, alpines
Shrubs, climbers (softwood cuttings)

John Hutchinson

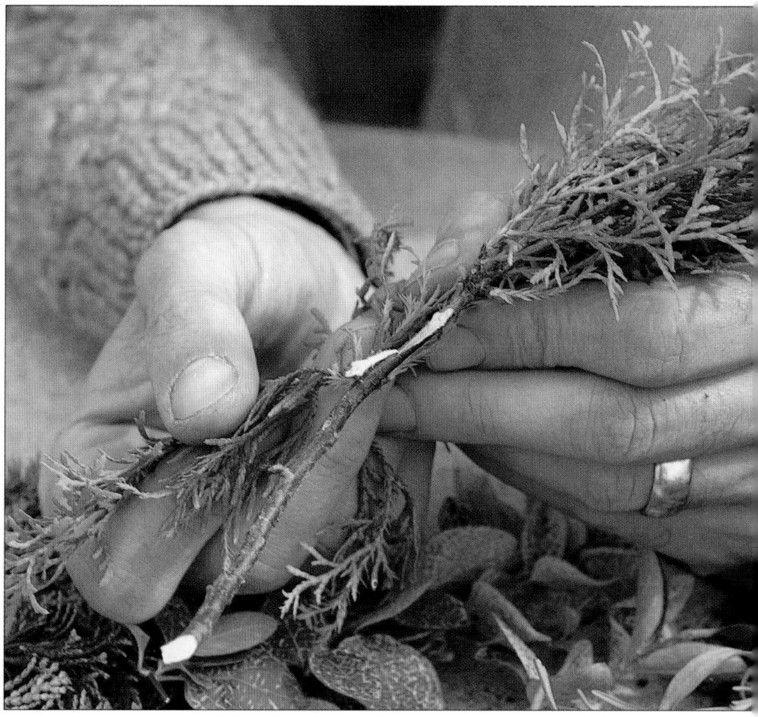

Photos Horticultural

LAVENDER FROM CUTTINGS

Lavender is easy to propagate from cuttings, and you can easily make a hedge of it from cuttings taken the previous season. Follow these easy steps to make your hedge. The cuttings will take about three weeks to root. Once this has happened, remove the polythene and gradually reaccustom your plantlets to full sun. Keep them indoors on a cold window sill (or in a cold frame) over winter. In the early spring, pot up the plants individually into 8cm/3in pots and plant them out about two months later, after hardening off. In well-drained soils, lavender flowers from mid-summer to autumn.

1 *In late summer collect lavender cuttings 7.5cm/3in long. These should be the tips of non-flowering shoots.*

2 *Use a sharp knife to cut through the base just below a leaf joint, remove the leaves from lower third.*

3 *Dip the cuttings in a fungicide solution and shake off the excess. Dip stem in rooting powder.*

4 *Fill with an equal mixture of peat and sand. Make holes 2.5cm deep. Push the cuttings into the holes and firm in*

5 *Cover with well-ventilated polythene and put in a warm, light place. Turn the polythene inside out regularly.*

HORMONE ROOTING POWDER

GROWING TIPS

Hormone rooting powder is best used in the season of purchase. Many plants root perfectly well without it if the timing is right. The process may be slower without rooting powder, but do not let that put you off.

If you only want to produce one plant then experiment with timing, too. It is surprising how often you will succeed with a chance cutting offered by a friend on the spur of the moment.

longer length than you need. You can then trim them up properly on a table indoors. Always keep your cuttings in a closed plastic bag in the shade until you are ready to deal with them, to prevent wilting. Remember to collect a few extra cuttings, too, to allow for a few failures.

Sharp, clean secateurs are best for collecting all cuttings and are perfectly adequate for making the final trimming up of woody cuttings. Softer stems are best cut on a board, using a sharp craft knife.

Take semi-ripe cuttings with a heel and dip them into hormone rooting powder. Plant cuttings in individual pots filled with an equal part of peat and sand. Place the pots in a polythene bag tent to prevent the cuttings from wilting and keep them in a shady spot (below).

Cuttings have a language all of their own and this may initially be confusing but in the end it all boils down to a few basic seasons for cutting: softwood cuttings are taken in spring, semi-ripe in late summer and hardwood in autumn and winter.

Softwood cutting

Softwood cuttings are made from short sections of new growth in spring. Take them as soon as about 5-10cm/2-4in of stem have developed.

In early spring take cuttings of the new basal shoots of delphiniums, chrysanthemums, fuchsias, achillea, dahlia and perennial salvias. In early summer try tip cuttings (4-6.5cm/1½-2½in) of potentilla, deutzia and cistus.

Softwood cuttings should be cut cleanly to 6.5cm/2½in long at the leaf joint or 'node', using a sharp knife. Remove the lower few leaves by nipping them off with your fingernails or with a knife. Dip the whole cutting in a solution such as benomyl fungicide and shake off the excess. Then dip the bottom inch into hormone rooting powder and push the cuttings 2.5cm/1in into an

Cuttings from a pelargonium are inserted into a growing medium (above). Choose two or three good shoots and strip off bottom leaves.

Make sure cuttings have rooted before transplanting. Pull gently and if it resists it is rooted (below).

equal mixture of peat and sand in a shallow plant pot. Water well. Cover with a clean plastic bag and seal with a rubber band. (Alternatively put the pot in a propagator with an electrically controlled bottom heat at 70°F.) Keep in a light place but out of direct sunlight. Most cuttings should take root within three weeks.

Turn the plastic bag inside out every few days to reduce condensation and so minimise the risk of moulds developing. It also helps if you cut off the corners of the bag, to give just a little ventilation.

Root resistance

To test a cutting to see if it is rooted, first look underneath to see if any roots are visible at the drainage holes. If not, pull the cutting gently. If it resists well, it is rooted.

As soon as the cuttings are rooted, take off the polythene (or remove from the propagator) and give them a few days to re-acclimatize before you pot them up individually.

Semi-ripe cuttings are taken in late summer, when growth is slowing down and the new shoots are slightly firmer. In midsummer try

geraniums, heathers, deutzia, weigela, philadelphus, forsythia, potentilla, and dogwood (*Cornus alba*).

You can often just take a side shoot, and cut it off either at a suitable leaf joint or with a little 'heel'. This means that you pull off your new stem with a little piece of wood from the older stem still attached.

Semi-ripe cuttings are easier than softwood cuttings because the risks of disease are less. They are slower, though, and it will be next year before your new plantlets begin to grow. Side-shoots are taken from the parent plant, from 10-20cm/4-8in long (2.5cm/1in in the case of heathers). Remove the leaves from the lower 5cm/2in of stem which is cut cleanly at a leaf-joint or with a heel. Dip the lower part into hormone rooting powder, and insert the cuttings into a pot of an equal mixture of peat and sand or into soil in a cold frame. Water well.

Stop wilting

A polythene bag tent over the pots will prevent your cuttings wilting, but they will still need shading from bright sunshine. Pots kept indoors on a window sill should root in 3-5 weeks and can be overwintered in a cool garage after their leaves drop, ready for potting up in spring.

Cuttings in soil in pots or a cold frame may not root until well into the winter, and are often best left undisturbed until the following autumn.

Hardwood cuttings are very easy but not all plants can be propagated in this way. In autumn try willows, roses, currants and cypresses. Simply cut off 23cm/9in lengths of good vigorous stem, and insert them into the soil for three-quarters of their length. You can either grow them in their final position or in an unused corner to be transferred the following autumn. Rooting takes place in the spring.

NO ROOTS

Q Last winter I took some cuttings to make a Leylandii hedge. Four months later they have not rooted. Is this right?

A Yes. Evergreens and conifers are slow to make roots. Just leave them alone in a cool place, out of direct sun, and wait. As long as they remain green, the chances are that they will root. Any that have gone black or brown should be removed. By next autumn the rest should have rooted. Because of their slowness, a cold frame is the best place for evergreeens, where they can remain until rooted.

WHAT WENT WRONG?

Marshall Cavendish

Propagating Plants by Layering

For beginners and experts alike, layering is a method of propagation which is almost guaranteed to provide plenty of plants for the garden or indoors.

Eric Crichton

It is easy to propagate strawberries by potting up runners while they are still attached to the plant. When roots have formed, the runner can be severed. Plants in strawberry barrels (above) will produce runners at a variety of heights, so pots often need to be propped up on bricks.

Layering involves rooting a shoot or stem while it is still attached to the parent plant. Unlike the alternative of taking cuttings, there is little risk of the shoot dying before it has formed roots. As the process requires only simple preparation and aftercare, this makes layering one of the easiest and most reliable methods of plant propagation for the newcomer to gardening.

It is one of nature's own methods of propagation. Shoots of brambles, for instance, root into the soil at their tips. The branches of some trees, such as beech, will often take root where they sweep to the ground, and stems of rhododendron will root and form new plants at the point where they come into contact with the soil.

Why layer?

There are many good reasons for layering. The main one is that some shrubs and trees are very difficult to propagate by other means, such as cuttings, but prove easy from layers. Examples include rhododendrons, magnolias, witch hazel (*Hamamelis*), camellias, pieris, elaeagnus and hollies (*Ilex*).

With certain plants, such as strawberries, this is perhaps the only practical way to propagate new stock.

Layering requires very little equipment or expertise and needs no artificial heat (except when layering houseplants).

The usual method for shrubs is simple layering. This is suitable not only for those which are difficult to propagate from cuttings, but also for virtually any shrub or climber whose stems can be brought into contact with the soil.

Carry out layering during the growing season, ideally between mid-spring and late summer. Use young shoots produced in the current or previous season, as old woody ones will fail to root, or will do so only over a long time. If desired, several shoots from each shrub can be layered.

How to layer

First, the surrounding soil should be prepared by digging or forking it over to a depth of

ENSURING CLEAN CUTS

The success of layers where a cut has been made in the stem depends on clean cuts, as opposed to ragged ones.

Ideally, you should use a proper horticultural knife, such as a budding or grafting knife. The best ones have a non-stainless steel blade which should be kept really sharp on an oilstone.

Try to make a continuous cut, as this will ensure really smooth surfaces to the tongue, which is then more liable to form roots. Jerky cuts result in ragged tongues which may not then produce roots.

Collections/Patrick Johns

30cm/12in. Mix in some coarse horticultural sand and moist sphagnum peat or coconut fibre. Break the soil down as finely as possible.

The shoot is prepared about 30cm/12in from its tip by first stripping off some leaves to make a clear section of stem. Then, in this area, cut a tongue about 5cm/2in in length by drawing a knife half-way through the stem. Make the cut through a leaf joint (also known as a 'node').

Wedge the tongue open with a small piece of wood or a stone and dust the surface of the cut with a proprietary hormone rooting powder.

The prepared part of the stem is then pegged down into a 15cm/6in deep, saucer-shaped hole in the prepared soil. Hold it in place with a piece of thick galvanized wire bent to the shape of a hairpin, and make sure the cut is still open. The top part of the shoot beyond the cut should be tied vertically to a short bamboo cane so it grows upwards.

Cover the pegged part of the stem with a 15cm/6in layer of soil and firm it lightly. The soil around layered stems should be kept moist until they have formed a good root system.

Gradual growth

Rooting will take place where the cut was made in the stem. Layers should not be lifted until a substantial root system has formed. This process may take as little as a year with some shrubs, such as forsythia, but can take 18 to 24 months with some of the more difficult shrubs. If you lift a layer and find that it has not rooted, replant it straight away and firm it in.

Lift the layers in autumn or early spring carefully, using a garden fork. If well rooted, cut away from the parent plant just beyond the roots. Rooted layers of shrubs should be immediately replanted elsewhere in the garden. Either put them in their permanent positions or, if you have the space, in a nursery bed to grow on to a larger size.

Another technique

Tip layering is even easier and is used for blackberries and loganberries and for other similar hybrid berrying fruits that have long stems.

It is carried out in mid- to late summer, using the current year's stems. Soil preparation is precisely the same as for simple layering.

Simply bury the tip of the stem about 8cm/3in in the soil. If necessary, keep it in place with a wire peg.

Alternatively, tips can be rooted in 9cm/3½in pots containing a peat and sand mix. Sink the pots to their rims in the ground below each tip.

Tip layering a thornless blackberry (above). The tip of a stem has been buried in the soil and will soon root.

Rhododendrons (below) can be layered at any time. A small slit along the stem hastens rooting. Roots take two years to form.

Marshall Cavendish

MY LAYERS FAILED TO ROOT

Q I layered a number of shrubs about two years ago but they have not rooted, although I closely followed all the 'text-book instructions'. Can you tell me where I have gone wrong?

A The most common cause of layers failing to root is the soil drying out.

The soil must be kept moist at all times. In spring and summer and perhaps in autumn, too, you will need to water as soon as the soil becomes dry on the surface.

Do not settle for a 'quick splash'. Apply enough water to penetrate the soil to a depth of at least 15cm/6in.

Using a watering can fitted with a rose, water on at least 27 litres per m²/5 galls per sq. yd.

AIR LAYERING

Cut a slit 15-38cm/6-15in below the tip, between growth buds.

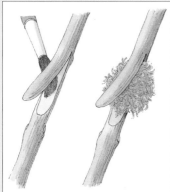

Dust the cut with hormone rooting powder. Pack with moss.

Enclose the cut with polythene, securing it at the bottom.

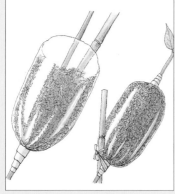

Pack the sleeve with more sphagnum moss and secure it at the top. Roots will grow into the moss. Tie stem to a cane.

Michael Shoebridge

In late autumn of the same year, when the tips have rooted, cut them away from the parent plant and plant them elsewhere in the garden. The best place is in a nursery bed where they can grow on.

Air layering

It is impossible to bring the stems of some shrubs and the branches of most trees down to ground level. These can be propagated by a technique known as air layering.

Prepare a young shoot as for simple layering, but hold the cut or tongue open by packing it with a wad of moist sphagnum moss, which you can buy from a florist.

Wrap more moss around the prepared part of the stem, holding it in place with a 'bandage' of clear polythene sheeting. Use waterproof tape to hold the polythene in place, making sure it is firmly attached to the shoot.

You should be able to see when roots have formed. Rooting will take one to two years. Treat rooted layers as already described. Remove the polythene but leave the moss in place; removing it will damage the brittle roots.

Border carnations

Many people are surprised to learn that border carnations can be layered. This is an easier and more reliable form of propagation than the alternative method of taking cuttings.

As the plants soon deteriorate, it is a good idea to propagate border carnations every couple of years or so.

The best time to layer carnations is in late summer, when flowering is over. For success, you must use the current year's shoots before they start to become woody. Several shoots can be pegged down around each plant.

First, lightly fork over the soil around the parent plants, using a hand fork. Then spread a 5cm/2in layer of John Innes potting compost evenly

Eric Crichton

over the cultivated soil.

Using unflowered shoots, carefully cut off the leaves at the base of the shoots, where they will be pegged down. Then cut a 3.5cm/1½in tongue in each, using the technique described under simple layering. Make the cut through a leaf joint. There is no need to use hormone rooting powder.

Peg down each layer into the compost, keeping it in place with a wire hairpin-shaped peg. The tongue must be kept open. Cover this part of the stem with a 5cm/2in layer of

Air layering is the most successful way of propagating any Ficus shrub. Taking cuttings is a chancy method, not least because they have to be propagated at a relatively high temperature, which can be difficult. Here (above) a cut has been made in a one or two-year-old stem in early to mid summer and rooting is taking place. The whole process, which is a little unsightly, may take two years.

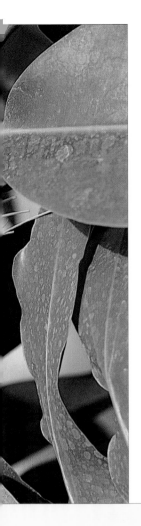

John Innes potting compost.

Keep the layers moist and they should root in about eight weeks. Cut them from the parent plants and leave them in the ground for a few days to recover from the 'shock'. Then lift them with a fork and replant them in permanent positions in the garden. These new plants will start to flower next year in mid summer.

Strawberries

Strawberries are propagated by layering the young plants which form on the ends of runners (creeping stems). Strawberry plants, like carnations, soon deteriorate and should be replaced by young plants about every three years to keep up crop yields.

If runners are not needed for propagation, remove them. Runners can be layered in early or mid summer. Always layer the first plantlet on a runner, removing any beyond it. Five to six runners can be layered around each plant.

Hold the plantlets in close contact with the soil by inserting a wire peg just behind each one. They can be rooted in the soil or in small pots of John Innes potting compost that have been sunk in the ground. Keep layers moist at all times.

When the plantlets are well rooted, in late summer or early autumn, cut them away from the parents and plant them in a newly dug strawberry bed. Flowering and fruiting will start the following year.

Indoor uses

Layering is not just a technique for garden plants. It is suitable, too, for some houseplants. Air layering can be used for woody or tree-like kinds, such as rubber plants and figs (*Ficus* species), crotons (*Codiaeum variegatum*), philodendrons, and dumb cane (*Dieffenbachia species*).

These are often air layered when they become too tall and need to be replaced with smaller specimens. You can do it in normal room conditions during the spring or summer.

Prepare a stem about 30cm/ 12in from its tip, as described for simple layering. The cut, which forms the tongue, is made in an upward direction. Dust with hormone rooting powder and then wrap the cut with moss covered by a protective polythene sleeve.

In warm conditions the stem should root in several weeks. Remove the polythene (but *not* the moss) and place the layer in a suitably sized pot, using soilless or soil-based potting compost. If possible, keep the young plants in warmer conditions for a few weeks.

If you wish, you can cut back the parent plant, by about half to two-thirds. It should then form side shoots and make a good bushy specimen.

SERPENTINE LAYERING OF CLIMBERS

Instead of obtaining only one plant per stem, you can ensure several from climbing plants by a technique known as serpentine layering.

Examples of climbers suited to this method are wisterias, clematis, honeysuckles (*Lonicera*), vines and jasmine (*Jasminum*).

This method is a variation on simple layering. Instead of rooting a stem in just one place, a long young stem is pegged down in several places along its length.

Climbers sometimes root more quickly than shrubs – often in as little as 12 months.

It is advisable to mark your layers with canes or plant labels so that you remember where they are. Make a note of the date so you know when to check them for roots.

1 Take a young, pliable outer shoot of the climber – here it is honeysuckle – and lay it out on the ground where you want it to root.

2 With a sharp knife make slanting cuts 1-2.5cm/¹/₂-1in long in the stem. Make the cuts close to nodes. Several cuts can be made.

3 Having added humus and sand to the soil, peg down each cut with a staple of bent wire and cover it over with soil.

4 Shoots layered in early summer should form roots by early autumn. Sever the plants, pot them up and plant out in the spring.

Peter McHoy

Techniques of Root Propagation

In many cases you can fill a whole border from the roots of a single plant in a short time. The method is simple and the results very satisfying.

The easiest way to increase your stock of herbaceous plants is to divide their roots. From a single plant, you can build up to a dozen or more in a couple of years with regular splitting. It really is a good, cheap way to fill a border, and groups of plants often look better than single specimens.

As well as dividing the crown of a plant, it is also possible to take cuttings from the roots of some plants. This is easy to do and is usually highly successful if you follow a few basic guidelines.

Divide and grow

The best times to divide herbaceous perennials are autumn and spring. Autumn planting allows just enough time for the new plants to settle in and build up their strength before they face the stresses of winter, while spring planting ensures the plants first face the world in warm weather. On cold, heavy soils, spring planting is generally more successful than autumn. Late-flowering plants such as Michaelmas daisies should also be left undisturbed until spring.

Methods of dividing plants vary according to the type of root system they have. Check what kind of root systems your plants have first as it is important to use the correct method. Looking at the roots will also help you estimate how many pieces your plant will provide.

A fork is the best tool for lifting out of the soil any plants you are dividing. You will need to resort to a spade only occasionally for really stubborn plants like hosta and aruncus. Ease up the soil around your plant with a fork until it comes free, with as much root as possible intact. Shake off the loose soil, and you are ready to start dividing the crown.

Fibrous roots

Fibrous root systems are the easiest kind to divide, and they usually break apart very

One of the most prolific herbaceous plants is Rudbeckia 'Goldsturm' (above). Its flowers have cone-shaped black centres. Flowering lasts until autumn and the roots grow quickly, which make the plant excellent for root cuttings.

FIBROUS-ROOTED PLANTS

Plants with fibrous roots will give you the greatest number of divisions per plant, especially when divided every couple of years. These include:

- yarrow
- lady's mantle
- pearl everlasting
- Michaelmas daisy
- bellflower
- chrysanthemum
- fleabane
- cranesbill
- avens
- bergamot
- phlox
- cinquefoil
- primula
- pyrethrum
- coneflower

easily. Simply divide up the crown into small individual pieces with their own roots attached. With some plants like anaphalis, bergamot and primulas, you can do this with your hands quite easily. For tougher subjects you may need a fork, or in some cases two forks, used back to back, as levers. The important thing is to take care of the buds and crown surface, because, although you can use brute force when necessary to divide roots, when you spoil the crown, the work will have been in vain. Replant the divisions straight away before the roots

have time to dry out, and water them in well.

Very leafy subjects like pyrethrum can be handled more easily in autumn if all the foliage is cut down to 5cm/2in before you divide. This also stops the plant wilting while it is establishing new roots. This is a useful tip for moving any herbaceous plant. Fibrous-rooted plants will give you the greatest number of divisions per plant, especially when divided every couple of years.

Some fibrous-rooted plants increase rather loosely at the root (Michaelmas daisy, Shasta daisy, Rudbeckia 'Goldsturm') and these are best divided into small individual shoots, as they will quickly build up again. Side shoots can be lifted without digging up the whole plant but you should lift and divide the whole plant every two or three years to keep it healthy.

Fleshy roots

Plants with fleshy root systems such as plantain lily (hosta), day lily (hemerocallis), red hot poker (kniphofia), and African lily (agapanthus), may be more tricky to separate into small pieces. Slice the crown in half with a spade and then lift just one half for division.

Washing the soil off the roots with a hose may make the crown come apart a little

DIVIDING LARGE CLUMPS

1 *Always be sure to keep as much root intact as possible when cutting under perennials. Try to keep the root ball firm when you move it.*

Both Photos Horticultural

2 *A dense root ball can be divided quite simply by using two garden forks, back-to-back. It is best to ease the clump apart gradually.*

Peter McHoy

The roots of the day lily (hemerocallis) are so thick and fleshy that it can be useful first to cut the entire clump neatly in half (left). This makes it easier to separate the roots, which should be done sometime between autumn and the following summer.

The rosettes of the saxifrage (right), can be detached and used as cuttings. This is best done in early summer. They will benefit from being grown in a bed of peat and coarse sand, with constant light watering.

Peter McHoy

DIVIDING IRIS ROOTS

The woody roots of peonies are storage organs, rather like a dahlia tuber. So, similarly, if you want to divide dry dahlia tubers before you replant them in the spring, make sure there is at least one bud to each division.

Rhizomes

Couch grass, ground elder and mint spread by enlarged underground stems, called rhizomes, often becoming invasive and difficult to uproot.

Solomon's seal grows from a much more restrained rhizome, which can be dug up and broken into smaller pieces, each with a shoot, in spring. It should be planted just below the surface of the soil.

The rhizomes of bearded irises live on the surface of the soil, where they can be ripened by summer sunshine to induce flower production. Divide these irises in the summer immediately after flowering. Every three years, lift the clumps and replant the best, strongest rhizomes. Discard the weaker ones and old, central, worn-out portions.

The rhizomes to be replanted should point towards the sun so the root is not shaded by the fan of leaves. The leaves can be shortened

The exotic beauty of an iris (above) appeals to gardeners of every taste. Wait until the flowering season is over before dividing and do not overcrowd the new plantings.

Lift those with fibrous roots with a fork and gently separate the thicker clumps (above) so that the root ball can be more easily handled. But do not strain the weaker roots.

Some irises have rhizomes; these can be pulled apart with your hands (above). Dip stubborn clumps in cold water for a few minutes and the soil will crumble away.

more easily. You can also shorten the roots to 15cm/6in or so. Replant at once.

Woody systems

With old woody hosta clumps, it is easiest to slice up the clump with a spade just as you would cut a cake.

Peonies, goat's beard (aruncus) and astilbes all have woody roots. In spring you will

need a sharp spade to divide old plants. Peonies must have at least one bud to each division, so you will not get very many pieces, even from an old plant. Unless you are especially keen to propagate from them, peonies, like hellebores, are best left undisturbed. Goat's beard and astilbes divide well but can be tough – so be prepared!

The Michaelmas daisy, Aster novi-belgii (right), has fibrous roots which grow quickly and benefit from being divided into small, separate shoots. If this is not done, the plant may lose much of its vitality.

PLANTS FOR ROOT CUTTINGS:

- Japanese anemone (anemone)
- bear's breeches (acanthus)
- anchusa (anchusa)
- stork's bill (erodium)
- sea holly (eryngium)
- cranesbill (geranium)
- Oriental poppy (papaver)
- border phlox (phlox)
- mullein (verbascum)
- tree of heaven (ailanthus)
- flowering quince (chaenomeles)
- Indian bean tree (catalpa)
- foxglove tree (paulownia)
- sumach (rhus)
- tree poppy (romneya)
- false acacia (robinia)

with secateurs to 20cm/8in, to reduce wind-rock until the plant is re-established. The species of iris such as *I. sibirica*, which have grassy leaves and thinner, drier rhizomes, should be split into small clumps rather than individual rhizomes, in early autumn.

Suckers

Plants which spread by suckers include rubus, Japanese quince (chaenomeles), tree of heaven (ailanthus), cherry

Patrick Johns/Collections

PROJECT   TAKING SIMPLE ROOT CUTTINGS

Taking your own cuttings can be very satisfying. You can use the new plants to add to the stocks in your borders or swap them with friends for their cuttings.

There could hardly be a better choice of a plant to take cuttings from than 'Drumstick primula' (*P. denticulata*). It flowers in colours varying from lilac to rose and deep purple, and looks attractive grown in borders, rock gardens and as an edging to ponds.

Its roots should be cut in winter when they are dormant. Cuttings taken in mid-summer will yield either a very low or no success rate.

Always leave about half the roots of each primula around the crown, so that you can replant it in your main display. The half you cut off will be quite sufficient for a good number of successful cuttings. These should be ready for planting by the following summer.

1 *Use a sharp knife to remove the thickest and longest roots. Cut the root close to the plant. Leave about half the roots around the crown.*

2 *Line a seed tray with a mixture of moist peat and grit. These should be used in equal volumes. Firm the mixture down with a tamper (above) or the back of a trowel.*

3 *Cut the roots into 5cm/2in lengths. The ideal thickness is that of the middle section. The ends, which are too thin for use as cuttings, are shown on the right.*

Marshall Cavendish

4 *Lay the good cuttings on the surface in parallel rows. Cover them with a layer of moist peat and grit. Leave the tray in a cool place while the cuttings root.*

5 *Wait about a month, until the new leaves are large enough to handle easily. Use John Innes I compost and plant them in 7.5cm/3in pots.*

(prunus), lilac (syringa), snow-berry (symphoricarpos) and acacia (robinia).

Suckers provide a ready means of dividing woody plants at the root. Separate the root from the parent plant at the point where a shrub has made suckers. This should be done between late autumn and early spring. Plant them as you would a new plant.

Sever the root on either side of the sucker with secateurs, then use a fork to lift the root. Sometimes it pays to sever the root a season before you lift the sucker, to make it fend for itself before you introduce a major upheaval.

Root cuttings

Some plants can produce new plants from cuttings taken from their roots, instead of the more familiar stem cuttings. They tend to be plants with fat, succulent roots which makes the process easier than you might imagine.

It is vital to keep the cuttings the correct way up or they will not grow. So to make this easier, cut the tops at right angles and the bases at a slant, so you cannot be mistaken. Root thickness varies according to the plant you are dealing with, but as a rule of thumb, do not use root sections that are much thinner than a pencil.

Cool places

Place the prepared cuttings 2.5cm/1in apart around the edge of a 12.5cm/5in pot of moist compost or soil, with the top 3mm/⅛in protruding above the compost. There is no need to use any rooting hormones. Cover them with 6mm/¼in of grit and place the pot in a cold frame or plunge it in soil in a shady garden corner.

Shoots should begin to appear by early spring, especially from autumn cuttings. These can be either potted up individually and grown on, or planted out directly into their growing positions.

Cuttings from the crimson **Chaenomeles** *(above) – a hardy flowering shrub often used to clothe walls – are taken from suckers in mid-summer and should each be about 10cm/4in long. Facing page: Shasta daisies (Chrysanthemum maximum).*

Harry Smith Collection

GROWING TIPS

SOUND ADVICE

Q How often should I divide my herbaceous perennials?

A The real answer is, only when they need it, which means when they begin to lose vigour and flower less well. For some plants, like bearded irises, Michaelmas daisies and Shasta daisies, this means every three years or so. Without division they would become congested, and the centre of the clump would begin to die out.

If you want to increase your stocks of a particular plant, though, it is quite possible to divide most species every year. The best time to divide perennials is early autumn. It gives them time to establish themselves before winter. On heavy, cold soils it is better to wait until spring.

EASY EDGING

The ultra-hardy and vigorous geranium *G. ibericum* is clump-forming but root cuttings could soon provide you with a natural-looking low divider for a cottage garden. It has large flowers and grows to 60cm/2ft high.

In late autumn, lift a strong clump of the geraniums; a plant which has been in your garden for two seasons or more will provide sufficient root material for 20 cuttings. Root in peat and sand mixture and overwinter in a cold frame or sheltered position before planting out. Space them 25cm/10in apart to allow for growth.

Marshall Cavendish

Making Use of a Greenhouse

Mini-greenhouses give an exciting new dimension to gardening. Learn what types to look for, how to look after them, and what plants to grow.

Few gardens are too tiny for a small lean-to greenhouse – sometimes called a planthouse. One can usually be fitted in against a wall or a fence, or even against the house.

For those with slightly more space, who prefer a traditional, free-standing greenhouse, there are miniature versions of the standard greenhouse – mini-greenhouses. They can be erected in a sheltered but sunny part of any garden.

Although small, lean-to and mini-greenhouses will help you grow plants that make your garden more colourful. They are also excellent for growing tomatoes, cucumbers and other salad crops.

Sun Greenhouses, Tamworth

Shapes and sizes

Planthouses (the smallest lean-to greenhouses) are about 60cm/2ft in depth, 1.5m/5ft to the eaves and 1.8m/6ft to the ridge, and in length they range from 1.2m/4ft to 1.8m/6ft. They have a sliding door at the front. Some have hinged ventilators in the roof area, while others rely on the door being left open to create ventilation.

Mini-greenhouses with a traditional ridged roof are about 1.8m/6ft wide, 1.5m/5ft to the eaves and 2.1m/7ft to the ridge. Lengths vary from 1.2m/4ft to 1.8m/6ft.

Standard-sized lean-to greenhouses are 1.8m/6ft to 2.1m/7ft in depth, sometimes more. A compromise between this and the smallest plant-

house – and one that suits many gardeners – is a 'compact' type about 1.2m/4ft wide. This has just enough space for a path and staging.

Unlike planthouses, in which plants have to be tended from outside, with the door open, the compact allows the gardener to work inside the greenhouse. This type is ideal for fitting to the rear of a garage, or against or even on a single-storey, flat-roof extension where you have access.

Siting the greenhouse

Lean-to greenhouses need an aspect between south-east and south-west; they must not be shaded by buildings for most of the day, nor overhung with

trees that create shade and drip water long after the rain has stopped.

Free-standing types also need a site away from shade and overhanging trees, as well as shelter from northerly and easterly winds. Orientate the greenhouse so that the ridge is east-to-west; this ensures that tall plants on one side do not

A compact lean-to greenhouse (above), at the end of an extension. This walk-in type has a sliding door at one end, a hard path, staging for pots and a bed below this for planting or putting down growing-bags.

A shelf (below) can be fixed at whatever height is convenient.

Sun Greenhouses, Tamworth

REDUCING HEATING COSTS

To save heating costs early in the year, sow half-hardy summer-flowering bedding plants on windowsills indoors. After germination – and when the seedlings have been pricked out – place the containers in your lean-to or mini-greenhouse.

Most seedlings take 7-14 days to germinate. Starting plants on windowsills indoors therefore saves two to three weeks of heating the greenhouse.

A mini-greenhouse (right), erected on a lawn. It has a sliding door at one end and a ventilation window on either side of the roof. For greater rigidity the aluminium frame is braced with struts on the sides and ends. Staging runs along one side and there is room for more on the other side, as well as shelving above it. The central area can be paved if there is not a hard base. This greenhouse is certainly small but a lot can be packed into the available space.

create shadows on the plants growing on the other side.

With free-standing greenhouses, it is equally important to position the door so that it is on the westerly side (or on the southerly end if it has to be orientated north-to-south) so that cold air is less likely to blow in through the door.

A flat, firm piece of ground is

A planthouse (below) in the tiny back garden of a modern house. This small lean-to greenhouse against a wall takes up very little space, extending only 60cm/2ft into the garden itself.

essential. One that slopes in several directions will strain the building, resulting in doors and ventilators that do not fit and producing unwelcome draughts in winter.

Mini-greenhouses usually have a path down the centre, and plants are put directly in the soil or in growing bags on either side. Lean-to greenhouses, however, are usually erected on concrete or paving.

Aluminium greenhouses are often supplied with an aluminium base surround that screws or slots together, as well as to the greenhouse. This is securely anchored to the ground by corner brackets set in concrete. Strong anchorage is vital, especially for free-standing greenhouses situated in exposed areas.

Heating

If the greenhouse is to be used to grow plants throughout winter – or for raising summer-flowering bedding plants in spring – warmth is essential. This is usually provided either by a small paraffin heater or by an electric fan or tubular heater.

The movement of air from a fan heater can help control fungal diseases. Both electric heaters create dry heat and can be controlled by thermostats. A paraffin heater produces humidity, which can encourage fungal diseases but is less likely to shrivel thin-leaved plants. If plants suffer from a dry atmosphere, place a tray of water on the floor.

Gas and solid-fuel heating systems are also available, but these are unsuitable for lean-to and mini-greenhouses.

Ventilation

Ventilation is just as important as heating – many plants are killed by excessively high temperatures in summer. If the greenhouse manufacturer offers an option of additional ventilators at the base and in the roof, take advantage of it.

The lower ones are often made up of adjustable louvres, while those in roofs are hinged windows. In free-standing greenhouses, try to have a roof ventilator on both sides, so that when ventilation is needed the one on the leeside can be opened. Whenever possible, avoid cold air blowing into the greenhouse.

Gadgets that automatically open and close windows and

STAGING AND SHELVING

Staging – a bench on which plants are placed – can be fitted into all greenhouses, even tiny lean-to types. It enables more plants to be placed in a greenhouse, as well as raising them to waist height where they can be more easily seen and tended. Two-tier staging makes even better use of the space, but remember that the lower shelf will be shaded and therefore may only be suitable for the storage of pots and boxes.

Once installed, most staging is permanent, but some hinges upwards to make it more adaptable. The surface of staging is either solid and perhaps made of plastic-coated steel trays, or slatted and made of fine-mesh plastic-covered or galvanized wire. In wooden greenhouses, it may also be formed from slatted wood.

The solid-surfaced type is better in summer, when it can be covered with sand to encourage the retention of moisture and humidity around the pots. In winter, however, when a better circulation of air is needed around pots to defeat attacks of damp-loving diseases, the slatted type is better.

Shelving is narrower than staging and is used to support pots and plants 23-30cm/9-12in below the eaves. In aluminium greenhouses, shelving is usually secured to the glazing bars by special brackets designed by the manufacturer.

In wooden structures, brackets and wires can be secured to the wood.

David Squire

louvres are available. They are often activated by heat-sensitive wax in a cylinder that exerts pressure on a piston. The device can be adjusted to make the ventilator open when the desired inside temperature is reached, usually about 13°C/55°F. The weight of ventilators varies, so be sure to buy an opener that suits your greenhouse.

Electric extractor fans (similar to those used to remove steam from kitchens) are another way to reduce the temperature. In free-standing greenhouses, install one in the glass opposite the door.

Summer shade

Small greenhouses are more likely than large ones to suffer from rapid and excessive fluctuations in temperature during summer. Apart from opening the ventilators and leaving the door open, shading is essential to prevent plants becoming scorched.

The simplest and cheapest form of shading is to paint a proprietary shading liquid directly on the outside of the glass. It is resistant to rain and can be scrubbed off in autumn. Unfortunately, this type of shading also makes the greenhouse dull when the sky is overcast.

Roller blinds attached to the outside of the greenhouse and formed of green, fine-meshed, weather-resistant plastic are better, as they can be rolled up and down to suit variations in weather. Alternatively, the plastic can be held in place with clips or drawing pins.

Conserving heat is essen-tial, especially if the greenhouse is used in winter and early spring to raise summer-flowering bedding plants.

Winter heat

Heat can be kept in by fixing 'bubble' sheeting to the inside of the glass, especially on northerly and easterly sides. It traps air between the plastic and the glass.

The bubble sheeting is held in place by a range of fixings, including double-sided adhesive pads, drawing pins and

It is important to shade plants in the summer. Here (above) an inexpensive, home-made green hessian blind has been hung from the roof vent.

Modern aluminium staging (below). Pots can be placed on the slatted metal top or, if the slats are removed, in a bed of damp peat or sand which will help keep them moist.

Sun Greenhouses, Tamworth

special clips that are made for aluminium greenhouses.

Both white and green 'bubble' insulation is available. The green often makes the greenhouse too dark in winter, although if left in place in summer it creates shade.

What temperature?

The range of plants that can be grown in a tiny greenhouse depends, like all other greenhouses, on its temperature.

Unheated greenhouses – often known as cold-houses – allow you to grow certain plants that you could not grow outdoors. Cool-houses, where the temperature never drops below 7°C/45°F, will extend still further the range of plants that you can grow.

Stove houses are even hotter – often 24°C/75°F and above – and are essential for the care of tropical plants. A stove house, however, is very expensive to run in winter, has unnecessarily high temperatures for raising plants in spring and is not needed for food plants in summer.

An agreeable temperature compromise – and one that saves money – is just to heat the greenhouse in late winter and spring, when sowing seeds and raising young plants. In summer, the natural heat of the sun alone will speed the growth of plants such as tomatoes and cucumbers.

Once your greenhouse is installed, you will want to pack it with plants. Both the time of year and the greenhouse's temperature influence the plants you select.

Starting off

The following plants and the routine are an example of what you can do in a small greenhouse heated in late winter and spring, but unheated from late spring onwards.

Raise half-hardy summer-flowering bedding plants to brighten flower beds and containers on patios. This is important to many gardeners.

During late winter and early spring, sow seeds of summer brighteners such as ageratum, antirrhinum, *Begonia semperflorens*, lobelia, nicotiana, petunia, marigolds and zinnias in 15-20°C/59-68°F.

After germination, prick off

Peter McHoy

A cheap but effective form of insulation in winter is to attach lengths of bubble wrap (above) to the inside of the glass.

An enormous number of seedlings (below) can be brought on in a greenhouse, for planting out later in the garden. This will provide you with an excellent, early display of flowers.

the seedlings when large enough to be handled into trays, seedboxes or pots. Slowly lower the temperature, ventilate more freely and by late spring accustom the plants to outside conditions. However, these plants are susceptible to frost, which in many areas may still occur until the first week of summer.

If a cold frame is available, place these plants in it from mid-spring onwards – covering with hessian on cold nights – so that the greenhouse can be used to establish other plants. Tomatoes in summer save on the food budget.

Growing tomatoes

Tomato seeds sown in 16°C/61°F in early spring develop plants producing fruit about four months later – sometimes earlier. However, as you will probably not need more than six plants, it is easier to buy established plants as soon as the greenhouse is free of bedding plants. These are best planted in growing-bags. A 1m/3½ft long bag accommodates about three plants.

Make sure the greenhouse is heated until frosts have passed. Supports are available for plants in growing-bags. Feed and water tomatoes regularly for a good crop.

Peter McHoy

Chrysanthemums

From tiny alpines to cottagey daisies and the handsome blooms of the show tents, chrysanthemums give us an outstanding range of flower forms and colours.

As summer beds begin to fade, the chrysanthemums come into their own. From late summer right through to the onset of winter, these magnificient plants provide a spectrum of brilliant colour that echoes the flaming hues of autumn.

Their enormous popularity is well earned. The diversity of flower shape and size from the huge, flawless globes nurtured for exhibition to the small, smiling daisy-like faces at the edge of a border, is exceptional, while their long flowering season and lasting blooms ensure a continuing array of almost every imaginable colour and hue. Chrysanthemums will grace borders, tubs and window boxes, as well as making good indoor pot plants.

Eastern origins

Chrysanthemums have been cultivated and admired in the Orient since 500 B.C., but it was not until late in the 18th century that they first came to Europe, brought from China by a French navigator.

In 1843, the Royal Horticultural Society sent the famous plant collector, Robert Fortune, to the Far East in search of new species, and some of his discoveries became the forebears of many of today's modern chrysanthemums.

The cultivation of modern varieties for exhibition is an exciting and all-consuming passion for a large number of enthusiasts, professional and amateur alike. These plants, though, are only part of a very large and diverse group.

The genus has been broken

Photos Horticultural

up in recent years, with species allocated to new genera, but, since these are not yet in common usage, we shall continue to love them as chrysanthemums. All have their individual virtues and delights, and all deserve consideration for a place in our gardens.

The modern garden varieties give us the greatest range of flower shapes and vibrant, jewel-like colours. They are classified according to the time at which they flower: early-flowering varieties bloom from late summer; late-flowering

from the middle of autumn.

Late-flowering varieties are grown in pots, standing outside during the summer then being brought in to flower in the greenhouse. In temperate climates, only the early flowers will bloom successfully in the garden.

Flower forms

Modern chrysanthemums are also classified by the form and size of the flower and whether they are borne singly or in sprays (see box page 1090).

Large blooms are achieved

PLANT PROFILE

Suitable site and soil Fertile, well-drained soil, in sun and with some shelter from winds for the taller varieties. Alpines prefer a gritty soil.
Planting Plant early-flowering varieties at the end of spring, adding plenty of humus to the site. Plant hardy perennials and alpines between September and April. Always give the root balls a good soaking before transplanting.
Cultivation and care Taller chrysanthemums need support in the form of canes or peasticks. Mulch early-flowering varieties in summer to help retain moisture, and water once a week unless rainy weather does this for you. Pinch out the growing tips of early-flowering and perennial varieties when about 15-20cm/6-8in tall to encourage lateral growths.

After flowering, cut hardy perennials back to ground level in early winter. Cut early-flowering varieties down to about 20cm/8in from the ground in autumn, right after flowering. The remaining stem and roots (known as the 'stool') must be lifted for storage in damp compost over the winter. Encourage new growth of stools after Christmas by providing a little warmth and moisture.
Propagation For early-flowering varieties, take basal cuttings from the stools towards the end of winter, and encourage rooting in a propagator. Established hardy perennials should be divided in autumn after flowering or in early spring. Take cuttings of alpines in early to mid-summer, root in a cold frame, then pot up in autumn. Seeds of annuals are sown on-site in spring and thinned out as required. C. frutescens is increased by cuttings of non-flowering side-shoots taken in early autumn or February and planted out after frost.
Pests and diseases These unfortunately seem to like chrysanthemums just as much as we do. Problems include aphids, leaf miners, slugs, snails and caterpillars, frog hoppers, earwigs, chrysanthemum viruses, mildew, leafy gall, leaf spot, verticillium wilt and rust. A system of regular spraying should go a long way towards guarding against such unwelcome guests.

The public face of the chrysanthemum is represented by the extravagant blooms of the modern varieties (left), seen on the show bench or in florists.

'Pennine Gambol' (above) is anemone-centred, with several layers of ray florets surrounding a large, raised centre.

Korean chrysanthemums, like many others, are now classified as members of the genus Dendranthema. However, despite their obvious charms, few varieties are offered for sale under any name. 'Raquel' (right) is a rare exception.

through disbudding: all but four or five flower buds are nipped out, so all the plant's energy is channelled into producing sizeable blooms on stems reaching 1-1.5m/3-5ft in height. Though mostly grown for cutting or exhibiting, the reflexed form is excellent in the garden, shedding the rain from its downward-curving petals or florets. 'Brietner' is a lovely pink variety; 'Bruera' a superb white.

Spray and pompon chrysanthemums bring an invaluable abundance of smaller flowers to borders, and provide some of the best cut flowers for the home. They are generally shorter and bushier plants (though sprays can grow to

Photos Horticultural

1.2m/4ft) and are not disbudded since their beauty lies in the sheer number of flowers.

The sprays have various flower forms, while pompoms bear small, globe- or button-shaped blooms. Together they offer a kaleidoscopic range of colours, from the single bronze flowers of the spray variety, 'Pennine Tango', to the pink,

anemone-centred sprays of 'Pennine Gambol' and the yellow pompons of 'Jante Wells'.

Korean chrysanthemums are, sadly, not easily found nowadays but are well worth looking for, since they continue to provide colour when the early-flowering varieties are starting to look a little battered. They are bushy plants, growing to about 60cm/2ft and clothed in sprays of small flowers in gorgeous hues.

All these varieties need to be lifted and stored away from damaging frosts. There are species, however, which are fully hardy and happy to remain in the garden throughout the year.

Daisy flowers

Chrysanthemum rubellum is compact and bushy, about 45-75cm/1½-2½ft in height, and covered from late summer

Eric Crichton

The clear pink single blooms of C. rubellum *(or Dendranthema) 'Clara Curtis' (left) are so abundant, the dense, bushy foliage almost disappears.*

The feverfew (C. parthenium) is a perennial usually treated as an annual. Here (below) it is growing through a clump of irises.

At the other end of the floral spectrum from the showy modern varieties is the tiny alpine C. hosmariense *(right above).*

The pyrethrums may be found as C. coccineum, Pyrethrum roseum *or* Tanacetum coccineum. *The species is not encountered, but the colourful hybrids (right) are a staple of summer flower beds.*

The marguerite (C. frutescens syn. Argyranthemum frutescens) is a tender perennial, in demand for containers as well as beds and borders. 'Jamaica Primrose' (right below) is an excellent variety.

Harry Smith Collection

Harry Smith Collection

Photos Horticultural

through autumn with clusters of single flowers in a cheerful array of colours. One of the oldest varieties, and still deservedly popular, is the delightful 'Clara Curtis' which has lovely, clear pink, golden-centred blooms.

The Shasta daisy (*Chrysanthemum maximum*), a relative of our wild ox-eye daisies, has long been a popular garden resident, cherished for its large white flowers borne singly through summer. Sometimes classified as *C.* × *superbum*, 'Wirral Supreme' and 'Esther Read' are much-loved varieties with double flowers. About 1m/3ft tall, Shasta daisies look splendid with golden-flowered neighbours.

Chrysanthemum coccineum is more commonly known as pyrethrum (*Pyrethrum roseum*). It is lovely in borders, with single or double flowers on long stems (60-90cm/2-3ft tall), and an array of colours from white through pink to red, accentuated by attractively feathery foliage.

There are even alpine species for rock gardens, such as *Chrysanthemum hosmariense*, just 20cm/8in tall, with white flowers set against finely-cut

Harry Smith Collection

silvery green leaves, or the even smaller, pink-flowered *C. weyrichii* (4-6in/10-15cm).

Annuals

Annuals, of course, are invaluable for adding shots of colour quickly and easily. *C. carinatum* (syn. *C. tricolor*) provides stunning, rainbow hues and attractive, feathery foliage. The flat, daisy-like, summer flowers, borne singly on erect stems 60cm/2ft tall have dark purplish centres surrounded by ray petals decorated with concentric rings of contrasting colours. 'Court Jesters' gives large flowers with a magnificent colour range.

Though a perennial, feverfew (*C. parthenium* syn. *Matricaria eximia*) is short-lived, and commonly grown as an annual. 'Aureum' is a lovely variety with fragrant, golden tinted foliage and small, daisy-like white flowers in summer and early autumn. A bushy plant, 20-45cm/8-18in high, it makes a neat edging for bor-

Peter McHoy

'Phyllis Smith' (above) is a variety of C. maximum with particularly ragged ray florets and a handsome, golden, central dome.

'Bronze Fairie' (left) is an early-flowering modern variety which boasts perfectly formed pompon blooms that are just 4cm/1½in across.

'Yvonne Arnaud' (right) is another modern early flowering variety. This time the flowers are reflexed, and much larger than those of 'Bronze Fairie', reaching 12cm/5in in diameter.

PERFECT PARTNERS

Jolly 'Court Jesters', with their multi-coloured flowers, do not fit into formal schemes and are best used in a riotous mixed bed with other annuals like nicotiana and mignonette.

ders and a splendidly decorative addition to containers.

The marguerite (*C. frutescens*, syn. *Argyranthemum frutescens*) has recently seen a revival in popularity, and is another excellent choice for tubs and containers, bearing a profusion of white, yellow or pink daisies through summer and into autumn.

Chrysanthemum care

While those who grow chrysanthemums for exhibition have their own recipes for success, there is really no mystery surrounding these versatile plants in the garden. They like sun and fertile, well-drained soil, and dislike very acid and waterlogged sites. Some shelter from winds is helpful for the taller varieties which also benefit from support with canes or peasticks. Chrysanthemums are prone to a number of pests and diseases, but regular spraying should take care of these.

After flowering, cut all the hardy perennial chrysanthemums back to ground level.

Early-flowering modern varieties need a little more attention. Plant them out once the danger of severe frosts has passed, then, just under two weeks later, pinch out the growing tip to channel the plant's energy into its side shoots. These will produce healthy 'breaks' which will eventually bear the blooms.

The size of the flower will depend to a large extent on the number of breaks that are allowed to develop. In the garden, about four to six breaks produce the best results, so you should remove any others as they appear. For disbuds, also remove any side-shoots which emerge on the lengthening breaks.

In midsummer, the flower buds appear on the top of each break, surrounded by a cluster of smaller buds. Take off these smaller buds, leaving just the central one, if you want large blooms. After flowering, cut them back to about 20cm/8in, then lift for storage over winter away from frosts.

COVER UP

Chrysanthemum leaves can cause allergic reactions such as soreness or itching of the skin. If you think you may be affected, avoid skin contact by wearing gloves and keeping your arms and legs covered when working with them.

SAFETY FIRST

Dazzling Dahlias

Dahlias offer you dazzling colour all summer and into autumn, along with plenty of cut flowers – all with the minimum of care.

You could not choose more worthwhile plants than dahlias and, what is more, you do not even need a garden to grow them – dwarf varieties are ideally suited to tubs or window boxes on a balcony.

Dahlias are perennials, capable of living for a number of years, but they are tender, so cannot be left outdoors over winter. The first frosts of autumn will blacken and kill the leaves and stems. The plants form large fleshy tubers, which allow them to have a long rest over winter as they store food and water.

Dahlias are split into two groups: the dwarf kinds which can be used for mass planting or formal summer bedding, as well as for tubs and window boxes, and the tall border varieties. The dwarf varieties grow 30-60cm/1-2ft high and border dahlias reach an average height of 90-120cm/3-4ft.

The flowers, especially those of the taller dahlias, vary greatly in shape. Dwarf bedding types have either single blooms, with a ring of petals, or double, with many petals forming a ball shape.

Tall dahlias

The most popular groups among the tall dahlias include decorative flowered, which have double flowers formed of broad flat petals; cactus-flowered, with double spiky flowers; and semi-cactus-flowered, midway between the

Decorative dahlias, whose broad, flat petals tend to curve in slightly at the edges, are available in a dazzling range of colours (above), though there is no blue. Many of the double flowers are multi-coloured, such as 'Master Robert' (above, inset).

PLANT PROFILE

Suitable site and soil: full sun and any well-drained yet moisture-retentive soil.

Planting: dormant tubers are planted in mid-spring, at least 10cm/4in deep. Young pot-grown plants are set out in late spring or early summer, when danger of frost is over. Space bedding dahlias 30-60cm/1-2ft apart each way and tall kinds 45-90cm/18-36in apart each way, according to height (the taller they are, the more space required).

Cultivation and care: before planting, dig in plenty of peat, coconut fibre or garden compost. Give the plants plenty of water in dry spells to prevent the soil drying out. Check containers daily. Feed border dahlias fortnightly, using a liquid flower-garden fertilizer. Cut off dead flowers regularly.

To keep plants from year to year, cut down stems when they have become blackened by frost, lift tubers and dry them off thoroughly, then store them in a cool but frost-proof, dry, airy place over the winter.

Propagation: large clumps of dormant tubers can be split into smaller portions just before planting. Each division must consist of at least one stem base and tuber.

Pests and diseases: the main ones are slugs and snails which chew soft stems and leaves. Sprinkle slug pellets around new shoots or young plants.

Brigitte Thomas/Garden Picture Library

two. Flower size in each group ranges from miniature to giant.

Other popular forms include water-lily-flowered, where the blooms look like water-lilies; collerette, single flowers which have a central collar of contrasting petals; ball dahlias with blooms the size of tennis balls; and pompon dahlias, with golf-ball-sized flowers.

Dahlias come in almost every colour you can imagine. There are all shades of red, pink, orange, yellow, purple and white. Some varieties are bi-coloured, consisting of two contrasting colours; others have several colours blending into each other. In many dahlias the colours are brilliant and dazzling, but others come in quieter pastel shades.

Dahlias are divided into groups according to the size and type of their flower heads and, in fact, the shapes of dahlia flowers are almost as varied as their colours. Cactus-flowered varieties (above) have a shock of long, thin petals. Semi-cactus varieties have flowers of similar shape although the petals are slightly wider.

Collerette dahlias, such as 'La Cierva' (left), are single-flowered with an inner ring, often of another colour (as in this example). They typically display dramatic – some may say – melodramatic – colour contrasts. Collerette dahlias usually have strong stems, so they are particularly good for flower arrangements.

Compact ball dahlias such as 'Wootton Cupid' (right) have densely packed, almost tubular petals. This popular variety reaches a height of about 90-120cm/3-4ft with flowers 8-10cm/3-4in across and is a favourite exhibition dahlia. Pompon dahlias bear a close resemblance to ball varieties but are much smaller, being only about 5cm/2in across.

There are various ways of buying dahlias. Undoubtedly the easiest is to purchase dormant tubers in winter or spring from a garden centre, supermarket or mail order dahlia specialist. Young plants can be bought in spring from garden centres or specialists, but these may be inconvenient for some people as they cannot be planted out until all danger of frost is over; in the meantime they must be kept in a light, frost-proof place such as a heated greenhouse. You could also raise your own bedding dahlias from seeds.

Dahlias are fussy about growing conditions, but if

Photos Horticultural

S & O Mathews

Derek Gould

Dahlia enthusiasts tend to grow taller varieties in special beds; they can, however, look very well at the back of a mixed border (left), where their dense foliage provides a backdrop for smaller plants and their blooms add a crowning splash of colour. Tall dahlias do, however, need to be staked, as here, to support the stems as they grow.

these are right they are very easy plants to grow. Full sun is absolutely essential for strong growth and prolific flowering. In partial or full shade growth will be weak and spindly and few flowers will be produced.

Soil types

Most soil types are suitable for dahlias provided they are well drained – if they stay extremely wet, or pools of water lie on the surface after rain, the plants are liable to rot. The soil needs to be able to hold on to moisture during dry periods though, as dahlias are thirsty plants. In very dry soil conditions, growth will be stunted and flowering reduced.

The best way to prepare the ground for dahlias is to dig in plenty of peat, peat substitute such as coconut fibre, or garden compost before planting.

Containers such as tubs and window boxes should be filled with a soil-less potting compost, either peat-based or one of the new coconut-fibre composts. Dahlias are also greedy feeders, so before planting apply a flower garden fertilizer according to the instructions on the pack.

If all you want is masses of

The single-flowered 'Coltness Hybrids' (below) are dwarf varieties with lobed leaves and daisy-like flowers. Though perennial like all dahlias, they are often grown as annuals.

colour in the garden without much work, there is no doubt that dwarf dahlias are your best bet. They are also the first choice for containers.

Tall dahlias are best for cutting but they need more time spent on cultivation as they must be provided with supports to which the stems are tied as they grow. The best

GROWING TIPS

REMOVING BUDS

The largest possible flowers are obtained by removing some of the flower buds, particularly useful if you want cut flowers or blooms for showing.

Each stem carries a central flower bud at the top with two more buds below it. If a large bloom is required pinch out the lower buds, leaving the central one.

Marshall Cavendish

A FLOWER ARRANGER'S DREAM

Dahlias are ideal for cutting, producing a succession of flowers in summer and autumn that last a long time in water (right).

Cutting blooms regularly will also ensure plenty more follow. The tall varieties are generally considered best for cutting as those produce longer stems than the dwarf kinds.

Photos Horticultural

BEST OF THE BUNCH

These readily available varieties are among the very best and the most easily grown, all of them flowering profusely with the minimum of attention.

Dwarf
These are seed-raised types offered by major seed companies.
'Coltness Hybrids' (single, mixed colours)
'Gypsy Dance' (semi-double, mixed colours)
'Redskin' (double, mixed colours, bronze foliage)
'Sunny Yellow' (double, lemon yellow)

Tall
Red
'Doris Day' (small cactus)
'Pontiac' (small cactus)
'Rotterdam' (medium semi-cactus)

Pink
'Gerrie Hoek' (water-lily flowered)

'Vicky Crutchfield' (water-lily flowered)
'Wootton Cupid' (miniature ball)
Orange
'Jescot Jess' (small decorative)
'Kym Willo' (pompon)
'Symbol' (medium semi-cactus)
Yellow
'Clair de Lune' (collerette)
'Glorie van Heemstede' (water-lily flowered)
'Klankstad Kerkrade' (small cactus)
Purple
'Edinburgh' (white, purple tips, small decorative)
'Moor Place' (pompon)
'Winston Churchill' (miniature decorative)
White
'Hamari Bride' (medium semi-cactus)
'Matterhorn' (small decorative)
'White Moonlight' (medium semi-cactus)

supports for dahlias are the 2.5cm/1in square wooden dahlia stakes that are available from garden centres. Alternatively, you could use very thick bamboo canes. Before buying stakes, it is best to find out the final height of the particular variety of dahlia. You can then choose a stake that is a little bit shorter than the plant after being inserted 30cm/12in into the ground, so that is does not tower above it in an unsightly way. The stakes, one for each plant, should be inserted before planting the tubers or young plants.

As the stems grow, loosely tie in each one to the stake with soft green garden string, making a figure-of-eight loop around stake and stem.

Plant combinations
In the garden dahlias can be effectively combined with various other plants. It is important to grow them only with plants that need the same conditions.

These days many people grow all their plants in mixed borders of shrubs, perennials, bulbs and annuals. Dahlias can be included, too, with tall varieties in the centre or back, and dwarf forms at the front.

Dahlias look superb mixed with shrubs noted for autumn leaf colour or berries, such as cotinus, rhus, cotoneaster, euonymus and berberis. The

basically rounded or ball-shaped blooms of dahlias also contrast strikingly with hardy perennials that have spikes of flowers, such as delphiniums.

Dwarf bedding dahlias can be combined with other summer bedding plants. There are many combinations but an idea that works well is to have foliage plants like the silver-leaved *Senecio bicolor cineraria* (usually sold as *Cineraria maritima*) dotted among massed dahlias.

Dahlias can be used as a focus in the creation of a subtropical bedding scheme. For example, the main planting

can consist of dwarf bedding dahlias. Among these plant varieties of canna (Indian shot) and tender fuchsias, whose delicate colours and pendulous flower forms provide a delightful contrast.

Marshall Cavendish

'Doris Day' (below), a tall cactus-flowered dahlia with relatively small blooms, is one of the most richly-coloured red varieties available.

Glorious Sweet Peas

No wonder the sweet pea is such a garden favourite. It produces flowers by the armful and the more you pick, the more the flowers appear.

Next to roses, sweet peas must be one of the most popular of all garden flowers. Perhaps this is because they are easy to grow and produce masses of blooms all summer with a minimum of care and attention. Many have a delicious, strong fragrance while some are only lighty scented. All are suitable for cutting.

Sweet peas are hardy annuals – the plants tolerate frosts in spring, and die at the end of the year, when the flower display is over. Most are climbers and support themselves with curly shoots known as tendrils, but some are very short plants, known as 'dwarfs', which need no form of support.

Delightfully delicate

The flowers are distinctive, having one large upright petal and two wing-like petals. The range of sweet pea colours is enormous: scarlet, crimson, maroon, purple, lavender, blue, pink, orange, cream and white. You can buy named varieties in single colours or mixtures of colours.

Sweet peas are generally bought as seeds and the biggest selection is offered by mail-order. A more limited range is available from garden centres. You should also be able to buy young plants from garden centres in the spring, as an alternative to raising your own plants from seeds.

Another reason why sweet peas are so popular is that they can be grown in various parts of the garden, from containers on the patio to flower borders and even among the vegetables if you just want blooms for cutting.

All sweet peas, whether tall or dwarf, like a spot open to the sky with plenty of sun. The more sun they see, the more flowers are produced. Avoid the shade as you will not achieve the results you want. Any soil is suitable as long as it drains well and does not become waterlogged after rain.

Apart from this do not worry too much about the soil as sweet peas are adaptable. Do ensure that they receive plenty of water: some soils dry out faster than others, particularly those containing a high proportion of sand, gravel and chalk, so take special care with these.

The right soil

If sweet peas have a preference, it is for slightly limy or chalky soil. They like a deep cool soil if at all possible and this can be achieved by digging in plenty of bulky organic matter before sowing or planting. Moist peat, well-rotted

Drops of rain from a summer shower glisten on the delicate petals of this spectacular display of sweet peas (above). The colours blend in complete harmony, ranging from crimson to lilac and white to peach. Keep tall sweet peas tied in to tall stakes at the back of a border or even in the vegetable patch (right).

S & O Mathews

garden compost, or one of the new peat substitutes such as coconut fibre will do the trick. The latter are a bit more expensive than peat but highly recommended if you want to become a 'green gardener'.

Choosing between tall and dwarf varieties should be no problem as you can obtain both types from garden

Andrew Lawson

PLANT PROFILE

Suitable site and soil: Choose an open position with plenty of sun. Any well-drained soil will do.

Planting: young plants can be planted in the garden or in containers when about 10cm/4in high, during spring. Space them 15-20cm/6-8in apart.

Cultivation and care: dig in plenty of garden compost, peat or a peat substitute before planting. Pinch out tips of plants when they are about 10cm/4in high to ensure plenty of side shoots. Water regularly, especially during dry weather. Feed plants every seven to ten days during summer with a general-purpose or flower-garden liquid fertilizer. Dead-head regularly. Discard when flowering is over.

Propagation: Sow seeds in spring. They can be sown directly into the ground or containers, 12mm/½in deep and 15-20cm/6-8in apart. Alternatively seeds can be sown in seed trays, using a soil-less or John Innes seed compost. Place the tray on a cool sill indoors or in a sheltered spot in the garden.

Pests and diseases: Sweet peas are prone to slugs and snails so scatter slug pellets around them. Greenfly can be a problem and are found in the shoots tips; spray with a proprietary greenfly killer.

Recommended varieties: Dwarf sweet peas are available in mixed colours. 'Bijou' is particularly weather resistant. 'Jet Set' is particularly fragrant and carries large waved flowers in bright colours on long stems. 'Patio' is a lightly fragrant variety and is good for beds and borders.

Tall sweet peas are available in single or mixed colours. White or cream varieties include the fragrant 'Royal Wedding'. 'Swan Lake' is good for cut flowers and looks good in beds too. 'White Leamington' is pure white and sweetly scented. Scarlet sweet peas include the fragrant 'Air Warden', excellent in borders and will add a splash of colour to your flower arrangements. 'Winston Churchill' is a bright crimson variety.

Photos Horticultural

Marshall Cavendish

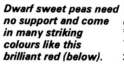

'Air Warden' (above) is an annual which grows up to 3m/10ft. The cerise-scarlet flowers are sure to create a sensation.

For a more delicate look go for one of the many pink varieties of sweet pea. Sugary-pink, salmon-pink, peachy-pink... the choice is endless.

Dwarf sweet peas need no support and come in many striking colours like this brilliant red (below).

Marshall Cavendish

55

Collections/Patrick Johns

There are a variety of methods which can be used to train sweet peas and each has its particular advantages. The sweet peas (left) have been trained in wire mesh columns. Plant several young sweet peas and stick three or four canes into the soil around them. Roll the wire mesh around the outside of the canes to form a column. Secure the mesh to the canes. Once the plants have grown fully they will hide the construction with their flowers and foliage.

PREPARING SEEDS

Sweet pea seeds have an extremely hard coating on the outside and this can delay germination. To speed up the process, soak the seeds in water for 12 hours before sowing, to soften them. Alternatively nick the seeds with a sharp knife, or rub them in one place with glasspaper, just enough to remove a small part of the seed coat and allow moisture to enter when sown.

centres and all major seed catalogues will contain a selection of each variety. The least trouble to grow are the smallest dwarf kinds as they do not require supports.

Tall varieties may be 1.8m/6ft and even up to 3m/10ft high. These are excellent for planting towards the back of a flower border. The tall varieties produce more flowers than the dwarfs, so are a better choice if armfuls of cut flowers are what you want.

Support systems

There are various ways of supporting tall sweet peas. In the flower border you could put up a 1.8m/6ft high wigwam of thick bamboo canes secured at the top with a plastic cane-support ring. The stems can be secured quickly and easily with wire plant rings.

Some of the most attractive-looking supports for sweet peas which are to be grown in

PERFECT PARTNERS

Eric Crichton

A beautiful combination in a mixed border consists of dwarf sweet peas grown in conjunction with tall white foxgloves, with their decorative bell-shaped flowers. The rose-mauve flowers of foxglove *Digitalis × mertonensis* would also look effective in this group.

a flower border are tall twiggy sticks. Tree pruning and cutting down large shrubs provide a good supply of sticks. They can be inserted in a circle in the border and the sweet peas planted or sown around the edge.

To form a colourful screen at the back of a border you may prefer to grow sweet peas on netting. Choose plastic pea and bean netting with a mesh size of 13cm/5in square, or a large-mesh wire netting. It should be 1.8m/6ft high and supported with timber posts at each end. Stretch galvanised wires between the posts and tie the netting to these.

Tall sweet peas can also be grown against sunny walls and fences (a good way of brightening up an unsightly garage wall). Support them with pea and bean netting, wire netting or trellis panels fixed to the wall or fence. If you have a trellis screen or a pergola in the garden this would also make an ideal support for sweet peas. For a spectacular effect allow them to intertwine with climbing roses.

Box of delights

Dwarf sweet peas are ideal for containers such as patio tubs and window boxes. They can also make a colourful edging to a flower border. Height ranges from 30-90cm/1-3ft depending on the variety. The shortest varieties include 'Patio' and the tallest 'Jet Set'.

The tallest of the dwarf sweet peas will benefit from a little support to ensure they remain upright. Use either twiggy sticks left over from

Eric Crichton

pruning or proprietary metal plant supports – the kind that encircle clumps of plants. Both types of support should be inserted before the plants become too tall – ideally when they are about 10cm/4in high.

Containers for dwarf sweet peas should be filled with a suitable potting compost. This can be a light-weight peat-based or soil-less type, or one of the new peat alternatives. You might prefer to use the traditional John Innes potting compost No. 1.

Regular checks

Sweet peas need plenty of water to grow well – the soil must be kept permanently moist and not allowed to dry out. You will need to check containers daily, or even twice a day in hot weather.

When watering make sure you apply enough, so that it actually runs out of the bottom of the container. Then you will know that the entire depth of compost has been moistened.

Sweet peas are great as cut flowers and freshly opened blooms will last a long time in water in a cool room. The fragrant varieties will, of course, scent the room. In fact, you may find some of them almost overpowering! Pick the blooms with long stems early in the morning and stand them up to their necks in water for a few hours before arranging. Sweet peas do not need other plant material to enchance them, although some sprays of gypsophila in an arrangement can look very pretty.

Sweet peas need not be confined to the back of the border. Plant them beneath a window (above) where their wonderful fragrance will waft through the open window in summer. Grow them with oxalis and saxifraga for a delightful cottage garden effect.

To keep sweet peas looking lovely remove pods, seeds and dead flower heads as they appear (below).

Lamontagne/Garden Picture Library

If you grow varieties in single colours you will be able to co-ordinate your sweet pea arrangements with the colour schemes of your rooms. Cut blooms regularly to ensure continuous flowering.

In the garden sweet peas combine beautifully with many kinds of plants. They will be 'at home' in mixed borders with shrubs, perennials and other annuals. They look particularly good growing with climbing or tall shrub roses. They could be grown through a large shrub that has flowered earlier in the year and which otherwise would look dull and uninteresting throughout summer, such as a spring-flowering forsythia.

Complementary plants

Sweet peas provide a tranquil cottage garden atmosphere, especially if grown alongside flowers such as roses, delphiniums, hollyhocks, honeysuckle, sweet Williams, Canterbury bells, foxgloves and mulleins.

In a more formal garden, silver-foliage summer bedding plants like *Senecio cineraria* make a good foil for dwarf sweet peas. Grow them in containers such as tubs, window boxes and hanging baskets.

Poppies

Bright, beautiful poppies create vibrant, eye-catching colour and bring a lively touch to both town and country gardens.

Photos Horticultural

Perhaps one of the most evocative of all flowers, the poppy *(Papaver)* captivates the heart and eye of even the most reluctant of gardeners. The romantics may picture country fields of swaying corn flushed red with hue of fragile wild poppies. The more stylistically inclined may imagine an oriental extravaganza of bold colours and textures. Whichever type you are, there is a poppy to suit you and your garden, whether in the town or country, formal or informal.

Bursting with colour

The range of richly coloured poppies is wide and includes many hardy annuals, a few biennials and some herbaceous perennials.

Introduce poppies which will complement your garden features. If you have a rock garden, try nestling a few alpine poppies against a large rock. The green-grey leaves are surmounted by flowers in white, yellow, red and orange and make a stunning contrast with the stark rocks.

Rockery poppies

A thin layer of shingle over the compost in the rockery creates further interest. It contrasts with both the flowers and deeply notched leaves, as well as preventing soil splashing on them during heavy rain.

The vibrancy of colour in a border of hardy annuals can be further enhanced by the field poppy, a hardy annual with richly coloured flowers. Keep the patches relatively small,

Of all field poppies, the variety Papaver rhoeas 'Shirley Single Mixed' (above) is the most popular. It is perfect for any wild-flower garden. Borne on slender stems, the petals look as if they are painted in watercolours, the delicate shades intensifying towards the edges.

The oriental poppy, P. orientale 'Diana' (left), has a flower so exquisite it seems to have been made from tissue paper. Set on a tall, thick stem the rich pink petals are blotched with black at the base.

as they can soon overwhelm less colourful flowers.

The oriental poppy is best suited to permanent borders and especially those with a rustic aura. These plants have a slightly sprawling nature that enables them to harmonize easily with old brick paths and walls.

Floppy poppies

Towards the end of the summer clumps of oriental poppy can become rather unsightly. They are therefore best planted with other plants in front of them to hide their sprawling and flopping

PLANT PROFILE

Suitable site and soil: a well-drained, relatively light soil and a position in full sun are essential. Avoid cold, wet soils and heavy shade.

Cultivation and care: remove dead flower heads of hardy annual and biennial poppies to prevent seeds falling and germinating. With herbaceous perennial types, also remove faded flowers. This ensures that the plant's energies are directed into growth rather than the formation of seeds. Use pea-sticks to support plants, inserting them early in the season so that shoots grow up and through them. Allow herbaceous perennials to die down naturally in autumn, then tidy up by removing dead stems and leaves. Once hardy annuals and biennials have flowered, dig up and discard in autumn.

Propagation: sow hardy annual seeds 6mm/¼in deep from March to May in the positions in which they are to grow and flower. Germination takes 10-14 days. When the seedlings are large enough to handle thin them 20-30cm/8-12in apart. Biennial types are sown 6mm/¼in deep in light soil in May or June, in their flowering positions. In autumn thin out seedlings to 30-38cm/12-15in apart.

They can also be sown in a seed-bed and transplanted in autumn into their flowering positions. Take care not to damage roots.

Sow seeds of herbaceous perennial types 6mm/¼in deep from June to August. When the seedlings are large enough to handle thin them to 15cm/6in apart. In mild areas move the young plants into their flowering positions in October or November: set those of the oriental poppy 45-60cm/1½-2ft apart. In cold regions, wait until March or April to transplant them.

Herbaceous perennials can also be increased by lifting and dividing congested plants in March or April and replanting young parts from around the outside of the clump. Discard woody parts from the centre of the old plant and replant the young parts to the same depth. Increase oriental poppies by root cuttings from autumn to late winter during the plant's dormant season.

Pests and diseases: downy mildew may create yellow blotches on leaves. Dust or spray with a fungicide.

PICK A POPPY

Iceland poppies create stunning arrangements indoors. For a long-lasting display cut them when the buds are just showing colour. Immediately scald the cut stem ends in boiling water to seal them. The capsule-like heads of the oriental poppy are eye-catching when dried and displayed indoors during winter. Arrange these with other dried flowers to make an attractive, everlasting centrepiece.

The Iceland poppy, P. nudicaule (right) is a tuft forming, short-lived perennial which is best grown as a biennial. Between June and July few flowers can compete with this delicately fragranced, bright-faced gem. Ideal for rock gardens, these poppies come in a wide range of colours which will enliven the stark background. This variety is called 'Summer Breeze' and is vibrant orange with a splash of yellow in the centre. A slightly shaded environment will ensure the Iceland poppy thrives.

Harry Smith

There are no prizes for guessing why these stunning red and black poppies (above) got their names. The variety is called 'Lady Bird' and it belongs to the species P. commutatum. The flowers are up to 6.5cm/2½ in wide and appear in June to August on slender, elegant stems which are 45cm/18in tall. The striking markings are in fact there for a purpose. They are called honey guides and help bees find their way to the nectar in the centre.

nature. The opium poppy also has country garden charm, with large flowers atop elegant, long stems.

Going wild!

Wild and natural gardens can be enriched with poppies, as well as by many other native British plants. Many seed companies sell field poppies in individual packets, as well as in mixtures with other native flowers such as primroses, cowslips, field scabious, foxgloves, wild pansies, cornflowers and corn marigolds.

Most gardens have a bright and sunny spot which is ideal for a wild flower garden. Within a few months it can be bursting with colour. If you already have field poppies or opium poppies in other parts of your garden, collect the seedheads and, when ripe, scatter the seeds in this area.

Some perennial poppies

GARDEN NOTES

POPPY IMPOSTERS

Not all poppies are poppies! Many plants have misleading common names:
- Welsh poppy (Meconopsis cambrica)
- poppy tree (Romneya)
- plume poppy (Macleaya)
- prickly poppy (Argemone mexicana)
- Californian poppy (Eschscholzia californica)
- Himalayan blue poppy (Meconopsis betonicifolia)

2in wide. They are available in white and many shades of yellow, orange and red. This is a short-lived perennial which is best raised as a biennial.

Another short-lived perennial is the Iceland poppy (*P. nudicaule*). During June and July few other plants can compete with its slightly fragrant, 6.5cm/2½in wide, bright-faced, paper-textured flowers in a

Marijke Heuff/Garden Picture Library

tend to be so short-lived that invariably they are better sown, then raised as biennials.

The alpine poppy (*P. alpinum*) is superb in a rock garden, creating a dazzling summer display of flowers up to 5cm/

wide colour range. Plants vary in height, from 45-60cm/1½-2ft and in width, from 30-45cm/12-18in. Varieties now include a wide range of glorious colours including white, yellow, orange, pink, salmon and rose, as well as some fancy-edged types.

P. commutatum, also known as *P. rhoeas commutatum*, is a hardy annual with vividly

The notorious opium poppy (below) is swathed in an aura of oriental mystique. Standing tall on greyish-green stems 75-90cm/2½-3ft high they are ideal for the back of a border. The crimson petals are ragged delicately at the edge, and the underside is a beautifully contrasting shade of pale pink.

coloured flowers up to 6.5cm/2½in wide from June to August. Invariably it is the stunningly attractive variety 'Lady Bird' that is grown. It is so called because it has red flowers which have a black blotch in the centre – just like the markings of a ladybird.

The oriental poppy is one of the most eye-catching of all herbaceous perennials. Bright

scarlet flowers up to 10cm/4in wide are borne from May to June amid deeply indented, hairy leaves. As well as the scarlet flowers, there are many superb varieties in pretty colours including pink, white and orange.

The field poppy (*P. rhoeas*) is a hardy annual, familiar for its decoration of cornfields from June to August with its very

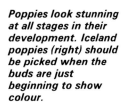

Poppies look stunning at all stages in their development. Iceland poppies (right) should be picked when the buds are just beginning to show colour.

The fluffy double-flowered opium poppy, P. somniferum 'Pink Chiffon' (below), displays all the stages of its development: the hairy green sepals open to reveal delicate pink petals, which in turn expose the seed head when the petals drop off.

Harry Smith

Harry Smith

Pat Brindley

bright scarlet flowers with black centres. In gardens it is equally attractive, with flowers up to 7.5cm/3in wide in an extensive colour range and borne on stems up to 60cm/2ft high from clumps 25-30cm/10-12in wide. The well-known Shirley Poppies are derived from the field poppy in a range of colours.

Another popular species for flower borders is the opium poppy (P. somniferum). This is a well-known hardy annual with dominant 10cm/4in wide flowers through the summer on plants 75-90cm/2½-3ft high and 30-38cm/12-15in wide.

Clever combinations

Plant poppies alongside other plants to produce a whole host of stunning effects. The rich colours of the field poppy create an attractive contrast in colour and shape with the narrow, mid-green and arching leaves of the feather grass (Stipa pennata). The silvery-buff plumes of this ornamental grass will arch and mingle with the poppy flowers.

Oriental poppies, border irises and clarkia (Clarkia elegans) together create a long season of colour. The clarkia is wispy enough to be planted

SPECIES AND VARIETIES

- Alpine poppy (P. alpinum) in a range of colours.
- 'Lady Bird' (P. commatatum), looks like its namesake, red with black blotches.
- Iceland poppy (P. nudicaule): 'Garden Gnome Mixed', with flowers in scarlet, yellow, salmon, orange, yellow and white, or 'Oregon Rainbows' in a wide colour range, apricot and peach, pink, lavender-rose, white-green with cream, pink and lemon.
- Oriental poppy (P. orientale): 'Black and White', has white flowers with black centres. 'Blue Moon' is mauve-pink with black throat markings and maroon veins, the petals

of 'Curlilocks' are ruffled orange-red, 'Mrs Perry' is salmon pink, 'Picotee' has a frilled salmon edge on a white base and 'Turkish Delight' is flesh-pink.
- Field poppy (P. rhoeas): 'Rev. Wilkes Mixed', semi-double and single-flowered blooms in many colours. 'Shirley Re-selected Double Mixed', in shades of white, pink, rose, crimson and salmon, and 'Mother of Pearl' in pastels.
- Opium poppy (P. somniferum). 'Paeony Flowered Mixed', large, double flowers in a wide colour range and 'Paeony Flowered Pink Beauty', double, salmon-pink flowers.

The alpine poppy (above) will nestle in a rock garden or grow happily by a wall. It forms tufts of grey-green deeply serrated leaves from which elegant leafless stems arise. They grow to a height of 20cm/8in, raising their sunny yellow faces to the sky.

The seed heads of the opium poppy, P. somniferum (right), are most suitable for drying. They make beautiful additions to dried-flower arrangements but are unusual enough to be displayed on their own. Cut the long stems of the seed heads and hang them upside down in a well-aerated, warm place until they are a bluish-grey shade.

Insight Picture Library

amid early and mid-season flowering perennials, where it continues the display into late summer or early autumn. The oriental poppy also creates a colour and shape contrast with the stiffly upright and grass-like gardener's garters *(Phalaris arundinacea* 'Picta'). The white-striped leaves of the grass contrasts with the up-turned, vividly coloured and dark-centred poppies.

Soft-coloured varieties of oriental poppies can be used with other pastel-coloured flowers to create an underplanting for pink, peach and buff-coloured roses. Avoid using strongly coloured poppies, as they will soon dominate the roses.

BEAUTIFUL BUT DANGEROUS

The fruits (seed-heads) and the sap of the opium poppy are poisonous, while all parts of the Iceland poppy are said to be poisonous. The field poppy is dangerous to animals if eaten in large amounts. If in doubt about your safety, wear gloves when handling poppies and certainly do not chew them!

DON'T FORGET!

PERFECT PARTNERS COLOUR CONTRASTS

Tania Midgley

A tall-growing opium poppy has been grown with Lavatera olbia 'Rosea', commonly known as tree mallow (left). Both plants flower through the summer. The slender poppy stems bear just one flower with a stunning yellow centre, making an interesting contrast with clusters of mallow flowers.

Poppies are at their most spectacular when growing wild in a cornfield (below). The bright scarlet flowers with black centres of the field poppy, P. rhoeas, add vibrant colour to the rural landscape in the middle of summer. Cornflowers provide a glorious touch of blue and mayweed a hint of white. Why not copy this effect by designating an area of your garden for wild flowers?

Nature Photographers

Geraniums For Borders

True geraniums are not as well-known as bedding geraniums – pelargoniums – but their delightful flowers and foliage earn them a place in anyone's garden.

I t is easy to get confused about geraniums; the name is given to two completely different groups of plants. The group that most people think of as geraniums are, in fact, impostors. The handsome red, pink and white flowers that look so well in pots, window boxes and hanging baskets, are pelargoniums.

To distinguish them from true geraniums, some call pelargoniums 'bedding geraniums'. Like other bedding plants, they are not hardy and must be replaced annually or over-wintered indoors.

True geraniums – members of the *Geranium* genus – are perennials that bear only a superficial resemblance to the tender, bedding type. Some books and catalogues refer to them as cranesbills or hardy geraniums. The name cranesbill comes from the long

Geraniums (facing page) have been combined with golden oregano and Rosa rubrifolia to create a colourful border. Geranium psilostemon syn. G. armenum (above) is an good all-rounder, its magenta flowers providing mid-summer drama.

65

Andrew Lawson

curved 'beak' of the seed pods.

Their shallow, cup-shaped flowers come in clear, jewel-bright shades of pink, mauve, purple or blue. Crisp whites are also available.

In some varieties, the foliage brings an added interest. Geraniums often have delicate, deeply divided leaves, attractive in their own right. There are evergreen varieties and a few that offer autumn colour when their leaves turn a glorious red or bronze. Some have aromatic foliage.

Friendly plants

Most cranesbills are fully hardy and will give you years of pleasure. A few do fall into the half hardy category, so check for hardiness before you buy.

They are easy to get along with as, once planted, they tend to require very little attention from you; they are not particularly prone to pests and diseases and require little or no mollycoddling. Regular dead-heading will ensure a continuous show of charming, jaunty flowers for a long period in summer.

The only condition that geraniums will not tolerate is waterlogged soil. Some like things on the dry side, others prefer more moisture, but all require decent drainage. They will, therefore, thrive in virtually any soil except unimproved heavy clay.

Although most geraniums like a sunny position, there are some that come in handy for more troublesome spots such as deeply shaded areas.

The glossy-leaved *G. nodosum* is one such plant, with delicate, cup-shaped flowers in tones of lilac pink to bring cheer to dark corners.

Another shade-lover is *G. phaeum*, whose soft green leaves and sombre maroon-

The muted colours and bowed heads of the shade-loving G. phaeum *(above) have given rise to its common name, mourning widow.*

The two-toned 'Buxton's Blue', also known as 'Buxton's Variety' (below), is the only commonly available variety of G. wallichianum.

Photos Horticultural

Derek Gould

Vigorous and long-flowering, G. 'Johnson's Blue' (above) is an excellent, clump-forming border plant.

The species form of bloody cranesbill (G. sanguineum) is veined with red, but the subspecies lancastrense (below) is a more anemic hue, with dark pink veins.

Gillian Beckett

purple flowers give rise to its rather sad common name of mourning widow.

Partial or dappled shade suits some geraniums best. *G. sylvaticum* 'Mayflower' is one candidate for such a position. Its cup-shaped flowers are a lovely violet-blue with white centres. *G. wallichianum* 'Buxton Blue', also known as 'Buxton's Variety', is a much paler blue, and its pretty white centre gives it a delicate air. It flowers from midsummer but is at its best a little later, when it gives a bright, fresh touch to the autumn tones surrounding it.

True grit

Some compact geraniums are at their best in rock gardens, alpine beds, sinks or scree gardens, where they appreciate the good drainage provided.

They have the added advantage of flowering in summer, when many alpines are past their best. *G. dalmaticum* is an excellent choice; it will drape itself elegantly over the edge of an alpine sink in no time at all. It has pretty, shell-pink flowers over dark green, divided leaves. The foliage provides winter interest as it is evergreen except in the harshest of conditions.

G. cinereum 'Ballerina' is a purplish-pink form which has lovely deep purple veins, while a subspecies, *G. c. subcaulescens*, has the most glorious magenta blooms. Both of these

S & O Mathews

SILVER LINING

The deep pink, purple, blue or magenta varieties of hardy geraniums look particularly handsome with silver-foliaged plants.

Lavandula spica 'Vera' or 'Hidcote' are a good choice because they bring a lovely fragrance. Their flower spikes contrast well with the softer looking blooms of geraniums.

Tanacetum haradjanii has pretty, feather-like, grey leaves that make a perfect foil for deep coloured geraniums. Rich pinks look good with it too. Remove the flowers as they appear as they tend to detract from the foliage.

Various members of the *Dianthus* family can be a good choice. Check that the flower colours are complementary before buying.

Andrew Lawson

With its low-growing habit and densely-packed, aromatic, semi-evergreen foliage, G. macrorrhizum (above) is a good weed-suppressing ground-cover plant; the same qualities allow it, as here, to tumble attractively over and down a low wall.

The meadow cranesbill (G. pratense) has a lovely, intensely coloured double form (left) which is known variously as 'Flore Pleno' and 'Plenum Violaceum'.

G. cinereum is an alpine species which rarely exceeds 15cm/ 6in in height. The purple-veined variety 'Ballerina' (right) is even smaller, just 10cm/4in tall.

PERFECT PARTNERS

The carpeting habit of many geraniums makes them a suitable choice for 'filling in' shrub beds. Here, *G. Pratense* 'Kashmir White' combines beautifully with *Rosa* 'Aloha'.

are suitable for rock gardens although they will also thrive in a well-drained border.

Bed and border

Geraniums make fine subjects for sunny herbaceous beds and borders, where they are useful as well as beautiful. Low, spreading varieties are ideal for softening the hard edges of paths, while taller varieties fill the gap between low growing, front-of-border plants and the giants at the rear.

Several varieties are excellent for the middle of a border. *G.* 'Johnson's Blue' for instance, will flower all summer long, bringing continuity of form and clear blue colour. It grows to a height of 30cm/1ft and a spread of 60cm/2ft.

The long flowering period of geraniums helps to keep things going in a border, filling the awkward gaps between spring and summer bloomers and between summer flowers and autumn colour.

Several varieties of geranium have foliage which gives good autumn colour and soft-coloured flowers which are invaluable when used as buffers between more dramatic plants that would otherwise make uneasy bedfellows.

G. psilostemon, also known as *G. armenum*, has a height and spread of 1.2m/4ft, so it needs plenty of room to display its magenta flowers with dramatic black centres and rich autumn tints. This handsome variety makes a good foil for silver-leaved plants.

The meadow cranesbill (*G. pratense*) can be invasive, spreading itself freely through the garden, but there are several suitable garden varieties, such as 'Kashmir White', 'Kashmir Purple' – these two are sometimes listed as *G. clarkei* – and the blue double 'Flore Pleno'.

Cover stars

Some varieties can be useful for providing attractive ground-cover. Their masses of handsome foliage will save you hours of work by smothering potential weeds before they can colonize your bed or border. *G. macrorrhizum* is an excellent choice for this job. It makes a low-spreading carpet of aromatic leaves and has clusters of pale pink or soft magenta flowers.

The bloody cranesbill (*G. sanguineum*) forms lovely hummocks of deeply divided, dark green leaves, crowned in summer with masses of beautiful, cup-shaped, deep magenta flowers.

Perhaps the most popular, and certainly one of the most widely available ground cover geraniums is *G. endressii* 'Wargrave Pink', with a dense habit and salmon pink flowers through the summer.

A spreading habit is also handy for bridging large gaps between shrubs. Geraniums with glowing magenta flowers make handsome, undemanding companion plants in a bed of old roses, for example.

Delphiniums

Picture an ideal cottage garden or a perfect herbaceous border; there, towering above it all, are the majestic blooms of the delphinium.

Delphiniums manage, somehow, to combine a regal charm with a cosy familiarity. They seem to be equally at ease in a humble cottage garden or in the formal borders of a stately home.

There are several good reasons why generations of gardeners have included delphiniums in their planting schemes. Hardy plants come in a whole host of reds, purples, pinks and yellows, but true blues are more difficult to find. Delphiniums offer a wide range of truly glorious blues, from the very pale to very dark, rich hues.

The stately shape of delphiniums adds to their appeal. They bring much needed height to the back of borders and to the centre of island beds, while their impressive flower spikes contrast well with the gentler outlines of other border plants.

Delphiniums are hardy plants, well able to survive almost any weather except drought and strong winds. Howling gales will play havoc with the very tall forms, so it pays to provide support early in the growing season by placing three 1.2m/4ft bamboo stakes in a triangle around each plant. Tie the stems in as necessary as the plants grow. Alternatively, commercial supports are available.

Dwarf delphiniums

Dwarf varieties have been developed primarily to combat the hazards of sites exposed to the winds. You lose very little in the way of flower spikes by choosing dwarf varieties, but the foliage is much more compact. In a very windy area it will still be necessary to provide some support.

Most delphiniums are perennial and are capable of giving pleasure for many years, though there are hardy annual species, the larkspurs, which are derived from *Delphinium ajacis* and *D. consolida*.

Blues plus

A wide range of colours is available, apart from the famous blues. There are dazzling whites, dusky pinks, subtle creams and rich purples as well. Recent developments include clear pinks, a salmon/orange and brilliant reds from the University Hybrid range of plants. With this selection to choose from it is possible to work delphiniums into any garden colour scheme.

Humble origins

The gorgeous hybrid delphiniums that we grow in our gardens today are the result of cross-breeding by keen amateurs, specialist growers and accidental pollination by enthusiastic bees.

The raw material for this work are close on a hundred species of wild delphinium that are to be found scattered throughout the world. Few of these wild plants are useful in the garden, as they are often insignificant to look at and difficult to grow. However, there are some species delphiniums available from specialists.

Gillian Beckett

In some delphiniums, such as 'Gordon Forsyth' (below), the flower spikes are 1.8m/6ft tall. Others, like the larkspur, 'Dwarf Hyacinth Mixed' (below right), are just 30cm/1ft. All of them make a strong vertical line in an herbaceous border. Different heights and colours can be used in a mixed planting to great effect (right).

PLANT PROFILE

Suitable site and soil An open sunny site with fertile, well drained soil is best. Will tolerate any type of soil as long as it is well prepared.

Cultivation and care May be planted at any time between spring and autumn, but spring is best. They like a well-settled root run, so prepare the site in advance if possible. Must have plenty of water during spring. Apply a thick mulch of spent mushroom compost or garden compost in early spring to help retain moisture. Feed established plants with a top dressing of blood, fish and bone meal in winter or early spring.

Propagation Experts disagree on whether or not to split crowns to increase stock. Taking cuttings in early spring is the safest bet. Cut young shoots 5-10cm/2-4in long as near to the woody crown as possible. Discard hollow or discoloured shoots. Plant cuttings in damp silver sand or vermiculite and place in a shaded cold frame or greenhouse. They should root within 6-8 weeks. Pot on or plant out in a nursery bed and move to a permanent position early in the following spring.

Sow seeds thinly on the surface of moist seed compost. Cover with a thin layer of compost. Cover with a lid or foil and keep at a temperature of about 60°F(15°C). Some seeds will germinate within days, others may take months. When sufficiently grown, prick out and plant in individual 5cm/2in pots. Remember that plants do not always come true from seed.

Pests and diseases Very susceptible to slug damage during winter and early spring. Cover crowns with sharp sand or similar in winter. Clear dead leaves and other debris from around your plants. Caterpillars of the delphinium moth are best removed by hand if possible. Mildew can occur; spray with a fungicide at the first sign of trouble. Good cultivation discourages mildew. Waterlogged soil may cause crown-rot. There is no remedy for this. Root out the affected crowns and plant new stock. It is good general practice to take cuttings of your favourites, so that you can replace them if necessary.

Insight Picture Library

Harry Smith Collection

RECOMMENDED

There are so many gorgeous varieties that it can be very difficult to choose. Here is a further selection to add to those already mentioned in the text.

'Rosemary Brock', 1.8m/6ft, deep dusky pink with a dark brown eye.

'Blue Tit', 1m/3ft, deep blue with a black eye.

'Sandpiper', 1.5m/5ft, gleaming white with contrasting dark brown eye.

'Gillian Dallas', 1.5m/5ft, very pale violet with frilled florets.

'Cherub', 1.5m/5ft, pastel pink.

'Fanfare' 1.8m/6ft, pastel blue, overlaid with a blush of pink.

'Lord Butler', 1.5m/5ft pure, clear blue. Makes a good cut flower.

It is possible to grow delphiniums from seed but the results are often disappointing. Hybrids are notorious for not growing true from seed and therefore you are best advised to buy plants from specialist growers. Reference to a plant finder should yield their names and addresses.

On receipt of their catalogues you will be astonished at the sheer number of named varieties available. Each nursery has a number of their very own, as well as the more usual types.

Where to plant

Delphiniums enjoy full sun and an open site. They should not have to compete for moisture with thirsty tree and shrub roots nearby. Their traditional home in a herbaceous border or an island bed is a practical and very effective choice of site.

If your garden is small, it is quite possible to grow delphiniums in large containers. You could manage to fit two or three dwarf varieties into a half barrel, for example. Plant a few trailing plants at the edges to soften the outline and a couple of pretty perennials and annuals to sustain interest after the delphiniums have ceased flowering.

The secret of success with delphiniums and herbaceous beds lies in choosing and preparing the site. The soil must be very fertile for large-flowered varieties. Although delphiniums like plenty of water, especially in spring, drainage must be good.

Preparing the site

Try to think far enough ahead to prepare the site in the autumn before planting in early spring. Although it is possible to prepare the ground when you are doing the planting, it is best to allow time for the site to settle. Delphiniums like a firm root run.

Bearing in mind that delphiniums need to be well fed and watered, dig plenty of organic matter such as well-rotted manure or good garden compost into the bed. This will ensure that they get plenty of nutrients and, paradoxically, will supply good drainage while retaining moisture.

Dig in blood, fish and bone meal at a rate of roughly 100g/4oz per sq.m./sq.yd. This will supply nourishment that is released slowly and steadily over the growing period.

Planting out

Spring is the best time to plant delphiniums, but you may have to wait until the following year for blooms.

You can plant in the autumn, which will ensure some sort of show the following summer, though there is a risk that more vulnerable varieties may succumb to very wet conditions in autumn and winter. This is particularly true if you have very heavy soil.

Some growers may not supply your plants until summer; you should plant them on receipt, but do not expect a show of blooms until the following year. The advantage of summer planting is that the roots can get established in warm soil. Make sure you keep them well-watered, especially in hot, dry weather.

Plant delphiniums in groups of three or five, as odd numbers tend to look less regimented than even numbers.

Although best known for the blue varieties, such as 'Lord Butler' (far right), there are many other colours in the delphinium's palette, including the pink of 'Langdon's Royal Flush' (right) and the pure white of 'Olive Poppleton' (below).

Insight Picture Library

Marshall Cavendish

Harry Smith Collection

Harry Smith Collection

CONTAINERS

If you have a tiny, patio style garden you can still grow delphiniums successfully in containers.

Incorporate plenty of organic matter with your compost and plant up with delphiniums and trailing plants such as ivy and lobelia to soften the outlines. Add some other favourite annuals or perennials between the delphiniums at the back and the trailers at the front.

Water regularly in dry weather. Remember to feed your delphiniums after the first year as they may be getting short of nutrients.

Michael Shoebridge

The popular variety 'Butterball' (below right) has white flowers, cream eyes and an overall greenish-yellow tinge.

Belladonna varieties, such as 'Lamartine' (below) have more widely separated flowers.

For the best effect, plant groups of the same colour or variety together. Plant them at least 60cm/2ft apart.

Spoilt for choice

There are so many really gorgeous named varieties on offer from nurseries that it is impossible to suggest more than a tiny proportion of them here.

Eric Crichton

'Olive Poppleton' (1.8m/6ft tall) looks well at the back of borders and brings drama to a scheme. This variety has pure white petals and a honey brown 'bee' or eye in the centre of the flower.

To bring warmth to your garden choose one of the lovely dusky pink varieties. 'Royal Flush', also sold as 'Langdon's Royal Flush' (1.5m/5ft tall), is a deep, rich pink with a white, contrasting eye. Grey or silver foliage plants will complement this lovely variety.

A cream variety such as 'Butterball' (1.2m/4ft tall) is ideal for a classic colour scheme of pink, cream and fresh green foliage.

Nothing quite beats purple for bringing richness to your garden. Purple mixes well with other colours, particularly yellow or white. The grey-eyed six-footer, 'Gordon Forsyth', is a good choice.

Famous blues

Delphiniums are rightly famous for their blues, which range from very pale to very dark. A deep gentian blue can be had by planting 'Fenella' (1.8m/6ft) or 'Nicholas Woodfield'; both have black eyes.

For annual delphiniums (larkspur) choose 'Giant Imperial' or 'Hyacinth Flowered' mixtures. Larkspur is better for cutting and drying then perennial varieties and may be grown from seed in autumn or spring.

Perennial Belladonna varieties are single flowered and branching, which makes them good for cutting. Choose 'Lamartine' for a violet/blue. 'Piccolo' is a short-growing, free-flowering gentian blue and 'Moerheimii' is white.

Radiant Sunflowers

Sunflowers, with their distinctive, brightly coloured blooms, have remained one of the most popular of the old fashioned flowers. They bring a feeling of naturalness and simplicity that takes us straight back to the good life.

Old world cottages, hazy summer days, and the sort of romantic countryside scenes depicted in Victorian watercolours – these are the natural settings for sunflowers. But even if you live in town, sunflowers, with their strong nostalgic associations, somehow still conjure up those same images.

Quite apart from their country cottage image, sunflowers can be useful in all sorts of garden situations. A row of sunflowers makes a good, fast growing, but non-invasive temporary screen, ideal for creating privacy in summer when neighbours are out in their gardens, or when summer holiday traffic is at is heaviest.

A row of sunflowers also filters the breeze, giving you a pretty but effective shelter belt within which to sunbathe, or to grow more delicate flowers which would otherwise be spoilt by the wind.

Groups of tall sunflowers look good grown at the back of a tall herbaceous border, or among trees and shrubs to provide 'architectural interest'. And for wildlife gardens they are invaluable. A huge range of insects will visit the flowers, and if you leave the plants standing after the petals have dropped, you'll be able to enjoy hours of aerobatics as the birds swing upside down while they feed from the sunflower's springy-stemmed, seed-laden heads.

There is even something for floral artists, who like to cut a

few perfect seedheads and varnish them for winter decorations.

Famous for their golden, dinner plate sized flower heads and their tall stems, sunflowers are firm favourites with competitive growers – many villages organize giant sunflower contests – and with schools for children's gardening projects, as well as ordinary gardeners in search of something spectacular.

There are perennial species, but the huge ones that most of us think of when sunflowers are mentioned are annuals.

The cottage garden is the traditional home of the sunflower, and there is no denying the appeal of a bunch of golden flower heads soaring out of a border (above). Here, the shape and colour of the flowers is echoed by the surrounding heleniums.

Brian Carter/Garden Picture Library

PLANT PROFILE

Suitable soil and site A sunny spot is essential for sunflowers. They will grow in any soil, but do best in rich, fertile soil that is reasonably well drained. Young plants can rot on cold, wet clay soil.

Propagation Sow seed in the garden where plants are to flower at the beginning of spring, choosing a mild spell of weather. Indoors, seed can be sown in pots from late winter on a warm, well lit window-sill.

Planting During mild, still weather in mid to late spring, when their pots have just filled with roots. Do not wait for them to become pot-bound. Knock plants out gently and tease a few roots out from the mass before planting. Plant to the same depth the sunflowers grew in their pots – deep planting can encourage stems to rot.

Cultivation and care Once established, sunflowers are naturally quite drought resistant, but for several weeks after planting, water them during dry spells. For best results, feed once a week with general purpose liquid or soluble feed.

Pests and diseases Rarely a problem in mature plants, though seedlings are liable to rot in cold, wet, heavy clay soil or a sunless situation. Small seedlings may be smothered by weeds if the soil contains a lot of weed seeds; if this seems likely, sow sunflowers in pots on window-sills instead. Mature plants sometimes get greenfly, but these are soon cleared by birds such as blue tits.

Annual sunflowers come in a range of warm colours and tones. The fiery 'Autumn Beauty' (above) mimics the golden yellows and russet reds of autumn leaves, while 'Sunburst Mixed' (left) is a seed mixture that provides a profusion of colour. Neither of these varieties grows as tall as 'Giant Single' (below), which has a 30cm/1ft-diameter single yellow flower head carried aloft on a tall, thick stem.

Young plants are only rarely sold in garden centres, but there is usually a selection of seeds which are so quick and easy to grow at home that it's a shame to deprive yourself of the fun, even if bedding plants are available.

Start in winter or spring by choosing your seeds. Between them, the big seed firms list a good selection of sunflower varieties in their catalogues, which are available free of charge from late autumn onwards; just write and ask them to send you one.

This way, you'll be able to choose from a much bigger range of varieties than is normally available in garden centres. Don't worry about the Latin name; it is *Helianthus annuus*, but the seed is usually listed as sunflower.

Flower choice
The basic choices are between single and double flowers, between plain yellow flowers or one of the slightly more unusual shades such as bronze, orange, white, mahogany or even crimson, and between tall single stemmed plants or shorter bushier ones which have more flowers, but of a smaller size.

For competition winning giant sunflowers, the variety to go for is 'Russian Giant' – one of the tallest sunflowers on record – which can grow to 2.5-3m/8-10ft or more. These are best grown against a wall, and ideally tied into place to keep them upright, especially if you want to grow a prize winner.

'Giant Single' is another tall one. At around 1.8m/6ft, it is

CHILDREN'S FAVOURITES

Young children find it difficult to sustain interest in gardening; things happen far too slowly for them. However, they are fascinated by the spectacular size and growth rate of sunflowers. The fact that they are so easy to grow makes them ideal plants for introducing young people to the joys of gardening. Encourage your child to join in when you plant and grow sunflowers, or set aside a section of a bed for their exclusive use.

BRIGHT IDEAS

RECOMMENDED VARIETIES

Russian Giant; single yellow flowers with yellow centres, 2.5-3m/8-10ft stems.

Giant Single; single yellow flowers with yellow centres, 1.8m/6ft stems.

Sungold; double orange-yellow flowers, 1.2-1.8m/4-6ft stems.

Orange Sun; deep orange double pompon flowers, 1m/3½ft stems.

Velvet Queen; medium sized single mahogany flowers with black centres, 1.5m/5ft stems.

Italian White; 10cm/4in wide creamy-white flowers with black centres, on 1.2m/4ft stems.

Sunburst Mixed; bushy sunflower with crimson, lemon, bronze and gold flowers zoned in contrasting colours on branching 1.2m/4ft tall stems.

Autumn Sunshine; yellow, bronze and red flowers, 1.2m/4ft stems.

Autumn Beauty; 15cm/6in wide lemon, gold, bronze and mahogany flowers with darker zones, strong 1.8m/6ft stems.

Sunspot; miniature sunflower with 20-25cm/8-10in wide single yellow flowers with yellow centres on 45cm/18in stems.

Teddy Bear; miniature sunflower with 15cm/6in wide double gold flowers on 60cm/2ft stems.

perfect for growing in rows as a tall screen or windbreak. Both varieties have single yellow flowers. And because all the plant's energies are concentrated into producing one huge flower at the top of that giant stem, the resulting flower heads are massive too.

Top doubles

If you fancy double flowers – highly spectacular creations, like huge, spiky orange or yellow pompons – then choose the orange-yellow 'Sungold', or 'Orange Sun', which has deep orange flowers.

If it's unusual shades you are after, try 'Velvet Queen' (mahogany with a black cen-

tre), 'Italian White' (white, black centre), or one of the multicoloured seed mixtures available such as 'Sunburst Mixed' (crimson, lemon, bronze and gold, often attractively zoned in a contrasting colour), 'Autumn Sunshine' (yellow, bronze and red), or 'Autumn Beauty' (gold, lemon, bronze and mahogany).

These 'fancy' sunflowers are ideal for planting in borders with a mixture of other flowers. 'Sunburst Mixed', being a shorter, branching variety, rather than the traditional tall, upright sunflower, is particularly good grown in the middle of a border, where it looks rather like a sunflower bush, with flowers at the tips of all the shoots.

More unusual still, how about miniature sunflowers? Nowadays there are some truly knee-high ones, small enough to be grown in pots on the patio, or by the front door. 'Sunspot' is a real baby, just 45cm/18in tall. Most endearing of the lot is the 60cm/2ft tall 'Teddy Bear', which has cuddly double flowers of perfect teddy-bear gold.

Easy growth

Sunflowers are extremely easy to propagate. You can either sow seed straight into the garden, where you want the plants to flower, or grow them in pots on the window-sill and plant them outdoors when they are big enough.

Sowing straight into the garden is the best method for those short of time, since you only need to prepare the ground, sow and wait. Choose a sunny spot with good soil,

GOOD EATING

Sunflower seeds are a prized food source for all manner of wildlife. This can be a blessing in winter, when tits and other acrobatic birds flock in to pick the giant heads clean, but a curse in spring, when birds and mice scrabble up the seeds as soon as they are planted. To prevent any disappointment, sow far more seeds than you need.

DON'T FORGET!

The complex flowers of the Helianthus give way to extraordinary spiral-patterned seed heads (above left) that are often cut, varnished and used in winter displays by floral artists. They are also appreciated by birds, who perform aerial gymnastics to get at the oily, nutritious seeds.

Among the most charming of the dwarf sunflowers is the golden double 'Teddy Bear' (below), which grows to 60cm/2ft.

A SUNFLOWER SCREEN

Although it is an annual, the size of a sunflower and its habit of growing straight and tall makes it a good plant for temporary screening. A row of closely-planted sunflowers will make a windbreak or hide an unsightly shed while a more slow-growing perennial screening plant is getting established.

Taller varieties of Helianthus annuus are perfect for the back of the border, and make an excellent summer screen or windbreak, especially when the stems are tied into a trellis (above).

Though the larger varieties are best left in the garden, the smaller, bushier sunflowers can make an excellent, long-lasting cut flower (right).

Gary Rodgers/Garden Picture Library

and remove any weeds. Then fork in some organic matter (peat, coco-fibre, or well-rotted garden compost) and a handful of general purpose fertilizer. Sow the seeds 6mm/¼in deep and about 7.5cm/3in apart in late March or April. When they come through, thin them out, leaving the strongest seedlings spaced 30-90cm/1-3ft apart.

Growing on sills

Growing plants on a windowsill takes more attention, but produces earlier and better plants without risk of losses — and if you want sky-high plants, it gives them a longer growing season to get really tall. Sow three seeds per 9cm/3½in pot of seed compost in early March. Water in, and keep on a warm, well lit window sill, but out of bright direct sun to start with.

When the seeds start coming up, remove all but the strongest in each pot. Plant them out into well prepared soil when the plants fill their pots with roots (you will be able to see the roots escaping through the holes in the bottom of the pots).

Whichever way you grow your plants, sunflowers will do best if you keep them watered in dry weather, and feed them once a week with general purpose liquid feed. And with very tall varieties or in a windy area, tie sunflower stems to stakes to keep them upright.

The Fragrant Garden

Delicious scents carried on warm summer breezes cast an intoxicating spell. Plant a selection of fragrant flowers for your very own perfumed garden.

known, easily recognizable fragrances such as rose, violet, honey, spice, lemon or mint. Smells can also be described as being sweet, aromatic, rich, heavy or pungent.

Many and varied scents

To appreciate fully the subtleties of fragrance, take the time to explore several gardens and familiarize yourself with the rich and varied world of plant scents. Experience the fragrances not only of flowers and leaves but stems, roots, bark, seeds and resins. Revisit gardens in the evening, as many scents are only apparent at this time of day.

You will find the rich and intoxicating fragrance of some plants wafting across the garden. Other plants are more modest about their perfumes, requiring you to plunge your nose into their petals or pinch their leaves before they surrender their delicious smells.

You will also discover that the most fragrant flowers tend to be in white or pastel shades, not dazzling colours; their scent attracts bees and butterflies. Happily, pale flowers

There is a feeling of tranquility and peace in the scented garden, a sense of timelessness. Sadly, however, fragrance is often the last thing to be considered when designing a garden, if it is considered at all.

A garden planted for fragrance is an unusual creation, but a delightful one. Different scents can be used to enhance and emphasize the overall character or theme of the garden. Colour may still be the most important design consideration, but by selecting scented plants that fit the chosen colour scheme wherever possible, you can add a whole new dimension to the garden experience.

In describing scents, we tend to compare them to well-

The sights and scents of summer are summed up by everyone's favourite flower – the rose. Its honeyed perfume is attractive to bees and butterflies as well as to the gardener.

harmonize well with less aromatic, brilliantly coloured blooms, allowing you to mix and match with different colour schemes. You can then create a garden design that is both visually pleasing and delightfully fragrant.

There are many different ways of creating your own scented haven or adding delightful pockets of fragrance to an established garden.

Scents can be confined to certain areas of your garden to create zones of fragrances and these can be separated by scentless flowers, so distinctive smells do not mingle. Each zone may evoke a separate mood or character.

Scents can also be used to

Wander down this camomile path (above) and each step you take will crush these sturdy little plants, releasing their peppery aroma into the air. Here it will mingle with the scents of the lavender and roses in the carefully planned fragrant borders. These are all old-fashioned fragrances that evoke the atmosphere of a typical country cottage garden.

reflect a particular colour theme. For instance, lemon scents are just right in a predominantly yellow garden, while rich, spicy aromas suit a garden full of deep purples, reds and golds.

Scented plants are particularly effective when situated beside a garden path or scattered around the edge of a lawn. On the other hand, you may decide to devote a small area of garden to scent.

Scented species can also be featured individually, so that a particular fragrance can be savoured in isolation. Rose gardens and herb gardens are often designed as separate areas for this reason.

Use the plan, below, as a guideline when planning a scented garden of your own. The area you allocate can be as large or as small as you like. An essential element, however, is a place to sit down and enjoy the fragrance.

The seat can be a permanent

PROJECT · A SCENTED GARDEN

Julia Bigg

The plan is for an area of garden 4.5 × 5.5m/15 × 18ft, but can easily be scaled up or down. The sizes and colours of plants are carefully varied, but this can also be changed.

1. summersweet (clethra)
2. three Ghent hybrid azaleas
3. sweet woodruff
4. lilac
5. tobacco plants
6. sweet alyssum
7. violets
8. chrysanthemums
9. phlox
10. peonies
11. artemesia
12. pinks
13. tree lupins
14. regal lilies
15. four shrub roses
16. mignonette
17. peonies
18. chrysanthemums
19. day lilies
20. pinks
21. fragrant viburnum
22. summersweet (clethra)
23. snapdragons
24. mock orange
25. daphne
26. a thyme lawn

Pat Brindley

Because of its heady, orange-blossom fragrance, philadelphus (above) is commonly known as mock orange. The pretty white flowers of this hardy deciduous shrub appear in clusters in early summer.

The clove pink is so named because it smells of cloves. This named variety, Dianthus carophyllus 'Cherry Ripe' (right) is guaranteed to add not only fragrance but a splash of bright colour to your beds and borders. Once cut, it lasts well in water, so use it in flower arrangements where its scent can be enjoyed indoors as well as out.

Marshall Cavendish

fixture, such as a bench, or you may prefer a paved area large enough to arrange deckchairs or even a garden table and chairs for al fresco meals.

Every element in the plan can be varied to suit your own garden. Replace the thyme lawn with camomile, for example, surround the seat not with low-growing sweet alyssum but bushes of lavender and add spring-flowering bulbs such as snowdrops and grape hyacinths.

Even the overall shape can be changed to a more formal layout with straight edges, and perhaps a brick path, or gravel, instead of flagstones.

Plant placement is a very important consideration. Plants that release their fragrances easily, such as roses, honeysuckle and jasmine can be located some distance from pathways and seating areas so their lovely scents are wafted on gentle breezes.

Most scented plants are not so richly perfumed, however, and need to be placed within easy reach. One of the most important considerations in planning your scented garden is ensuring that the plants are readily accessible.

Sit and savour

Plants with delicately scented flowers and leaves ideally should be placed near paths or seating areas where they can be touched or squeezed to release their fragrance. Plants

When the sweet smells of summer have started to fade, the citrus scent of lemon verbena is waiting to be savoured. Grow it in a tub (left) to be located wherever it can be most appreciated.

Similarly, night-scented stock (right) is best grown near a patio or terrace where you can sit on summer evenings and enjoy its strong scent.

Hollygrape (far right) is an evergreen shrub whose showy yellow flowers will enrich a winter garden with their sweet scent.

Derek Gould

Photos Horticultural

such as camomile, thyme or penny royal can be grown between paving stones or in a path. Their lovely aromas are released as you step on them.

Elevating the senses

Fragrant flowers are often the main attraction in gardens designed for the blind or partially sighted. Often, these plants are grown in raised beds so their fragrances can be enjoyed at nose level. Handling and touching the plants is encouraged, to release smells and to help develop an appreciation for differences in shapes and textures.

You can use this idea in your own garden. Try growing fragrant plants in raised beds, hanging baskets, containers and window boxes. Placed near doors and windows, their wonderful scents can be enjoyed both inside and out. It is a lovely way of enriching the lives of people who may have to spend a lot of time indoors.

Preserving the perfume

The fragrant mixtures of dried flowers known as pot pourri are commercially available, but when you have a garden full of scented plants it is more rewarding to make your own,

GARDEN NOTES

NIGHT STOCK

Some plants release their perfumes at night. These are perfect for a terrace or patio. Cherry pie has a fruity smell, but tobacco plants and night-scented stock are both strong and sweet. Evening primrose is musky while dame's violet smells strongly of violets.

SCENTED PLANT SELECTION

Make your own selection of perfumed plants from the following list, noting scent and flowering times:

Winter-flowering

wintersweet (*Chimonanthus praecox*)	violet
crocus (*Crocus chrysanthus*)	delicate
mezereon (*Daphne mezereum*)	violet
witch hazel (*Hamamelis mollis*)	sweet/strong
hollygrape (*Mahonia lomariifolia*)	sweet
viburnum (*Viburnum farreri*)	rich

Spring-flowering

lily-of-the-valley (*Convallaria majalis*)	rich
snowdrops (*Galanthus* species)	honey
iris (*Iris reticulata*)	violet
snowflake (*Leucojum vernum*)	violet
magnolia (*Magnolia* species)	sweet
grape hyacinth (*Muscari armeniacum*)	rich
osmanthus (*Osmanthus delavayi*)	sweet
rhododendrons and azaleas (*Rhododendron* species)	sweet

Summer-flowering

snapdragons (*Antirrhinum majus*)	sweet
pot marigold (*Calendula officinalis*)	pungent
hawthorn (*Crataegus species*)	sweet
clematis (*Clematis montana* and hybrids)	sweet/strong
pinks/carnations (*Dianthus* species)	sweet
gilia (*Gilia tricolor*)	chocolate
day lilies (*Hemerocallis* species)	sweet
lavender (*Lavandula* species)	lavender
beebalm (*Monarda didyma*)	sweet
regal lily (*Lilium regale*)	rich
phlox (*Phlox paniculata*)	sweet
mock orange (*Philadelphus coronarius*)	orange
salvia (*Salvia* species)	aromatic
lilac (*Syringa* species)	rich

Autumn-flowering

yarrow (*Achillea filipendulina*)	pungent (leaves)
southernwood (*Artemisia abrotanum*)	aromatic (leaves)
chrysanthemum (*Chrysanthemum* species)	aromatic (leaves)
crocus (*Crocus sativus*)	sweet
elaeagnus (*Elaeagnus pungens*)	sweet
jasmine (*Jasminum officinale*)	jasmine
lemon verbena (*Lippia citriodora*)	lemon
osmanthus (*Osmanthus heterophyllis*)	sweet
honeysuckle (*Lonicera japonica* 'Aureoreticulata')	sweet

Insight Picture Library

FLOWER ARRANGING

The following fragrant flowers last well when cut: Peruvian lilies
- pot marigold
- wallflower
- chrysanthemums
- hyacinths
- bearded iris
- sweet peas
- regal lily
- paeony
- roses

Surround yourself with lavender by planting it round a garden bench (above), or grow it in generous clumps alongside a path (right). Both leaves and flowers have a strong, very characteristic perfume. Harvest the flowers to scent your house or dry them to make pot pourri.

Marijke Heuff/Garden Picture Library

Harry Smith

If you grow tobacco plants in a raised bed, the aroma can be appreciated at 'nose' level. Colourful, easy to grow and shade-tolerant, they flower all summer long. The tube-shaped, starry flowers open up in the evening to release their sweet fragrance.

In this bed (left) a clump of trailing ivy, Hedera helix 'Glacier' softens the edge of the bricks and provides a soft contrast to the bright red flowers.

Mexican orange blossom (Choisya ternata 'Sundance') is an attractive shrub with glossy, bright yellow leaves that give off a pleasant, orange-like aroma when crushed. Planted with the brightly coloured Aster novi-belgii 'Audrey' (facing page), it looks spectacular.

and preserve the scents of summer all year long.

A basic mixture might include rose petals, lavender flowers, lemon verbena leaves, camomile flowers, herbs and scented geranium leaves.

The flowers should ideally be picked after a long dry spell, although not when the weather has been so dry that the plants are wilting from lack of water. However, especially later in the year, you may find that you have to make a choice between waiting for the moment when the flowers reach perfection and beating the first frosts and gales which could very easily ruin a whole year's work.

Harvest on a dry day. Wait until the dew has evaporated, but try not to pick when it is too hot as the flowers may be wilting or in the evening when they may be damp. Shake the stems to dislodge any insects hiding unseen among the petals. Spread the petals and leaves to dry in single layers on sheets of absorbent paper and place in a warm, dry place, out of direct sunlight. When dry, mix them together. Add freshly ground spices, drops of perfumed oil or essences, or pieces of dried lemon, lime or orange peel, if you wish. Put the finished product in bowls and scatter them round your home to bring a fresh smell of summer all year round or give them to friends and relatives as an ideal gift. When the scent starts to fade, revitalize it with a few drops of the appropriate perfumed oil or essence.

Wild Flowers In The Garden

Do your bit for nature and the environment by making room in your garden for some of our increasingly rare native species.

This carefuly contrived wild garden looks completely natural. Native plants like white and mauve dame's violets, blue cornflowers and bright red poppies are grown in bold patches, while yellow Welsh poppies and spikes of mullein have self-seeded. Heartsease grows in drifts, and daisies dot the grass. Once established, a garden like this thrives on a minimum of attention.

Imagine a summer's day in a garden of wild flowers, where all the colours blend into a pastel haze and the air is filled with the perfume of nectar and the humming of bees. If this is your picture of what a wild flower garden should be, then you will be pleased to know that making your dream come true is easier than you think. If, on the other hand, you imagine an invasion of weeds and a tangle of un-wanted plants, then it is worth thinking again.

Wild flowers are simply plants that, under natural conditions, would grow in the wild: these plants are our native species and they are all perfectly suited to the weather and soils of this country. Many of our traditional garden plants are descended from these native wild flowers. Cottage gardeners long ago would have grown only wild flowers because these were the only plants available. It was not until breeders began to select particular colours and shapes they liked, crossing native species with plants imported from abroad, that the cultivated garden plant was born. Over the years, more exotic species were introduced and some of our common wild flowers were forgotten.

Wild flowers are now back in fashion. This is partly because

Eric Crichton

This yellow and white colour scheme (left) has tiny daffodils (Narcissus), as well as the more common larger ones, with ox-eye daisies and tall buttercups growing among green ferns and leaves. The patch of pink campion at the back adds a contrasting note.

The nodding sky-blue harebell (Campanula rotundifolia) (below) must be one of the prettiest small wild flowers, and is perfect for a wild flower garden. Harebells will enjoy a sheltered spot in the rockery, and are ideal for wild meadow areas.

people are aware that too many plants are being threatened with extinction as their natural habitats are destroyed by agriculture and building developments. Gardens are one of the few safe havens for wild flowers, and by introducing even a few plants to your garden you will be helping to safeguard their future.

Pretty, easy plants

Conservation is not the only reason for growing wild flowers. Cowslips, daisies, columbine and primroses are some of the prettiest flowers to be found anywhere and you do not need any special skills to grow them. On the whole, native flowers are better for wildlife too, attracting a wide range of insects and birds. Last but not least, wild flowers do not need to be fussed over with intensive watering and feeding. They will grow strong and healthy in even the smallest garden, as long you choose the right plants for your soil and situation. You may even find that they grow better in the garden than in the wild places around your home.

The first step towards establishing wild flowers is to take a good look at your garden and see what is growing there. Look closely and you will see flowers that were not planted, but just 'turned up': daisies, clover and dandelions grow in the lawn, thistles and bindweed in the flower beds. Once you get to know and recognize these wild flowers, you can decide which you like and which you do not. It is up to you to decide which are your 'weeds' and which are flowers.

Good management

A wild flower garden, like a conventional one, needs management if you are to grow the plants you want, rather than the ones that just happen to grow. There is a myth that wild flower gardens have to be untidy. The truth is, you can grow wild flowers, just like any other garden flowers, in neat, straight rows if you want to, but to create a more natural feel they are best grouped together in patches, giving a pretty, cottage garden effect. If there is room it is also worth allowing nettles, brambles and

G.J. Cambridge/NHPA

TOP FIVE WILD FLOWERS FOR GARDENS

Bluebell *(Hyacinthoides non-scripta)*
The nodding heads of bluebells used to be common in woods and hedgerows but they are becoming less common now. They prefer a lightly shaded position; under a hedge or decidous tree is ideal.

TYPE: Perennial, bulb
COLOUR: Blue
PLANTING TIME: Autumn
FLOWERING TIME: Spring to early summer
HEIGHT: 30-40cm/12-16in
SOIL: Any

Common poppy *(Papaver rhoeas)*
One of the best-known annual wild flowers, the poppy used to be found in cornfields but is now more likely to be seen on disturbed earth on roadside and motorway verges. It can be grown in a sunny border or as part of a wildflower meadow.

TYPE: Annual, seed
COLOUR: Red
SOWING TIME: Spring
FLOWERING TIME: Early to late summer
HEIGHT: 40-60cm/16-24in
SOIL: Any, particularly on poor, stony soils

Cornflower *(Centaurea cyanus)*
Once a widespread 'weed' in cornfields, it makes a pretty border flower for cutting. It prefers a sunny position, where it will attract bees and several different species of butterfly.

TYPE: Annual, seed
COLOUR: Bright blue
SOWING TIME: Spring
FLOWERING TIME: Summer
HEIGHT: 60-90cm/24-36in
SOIL: Any, except chalk

Foxglove *(Digitalis purpurea)*
A native of woodlands, the foxglove thrives in a damp, partially shaded spot. This stately plant looks good grown under tall trees or to give height at the back of the border.

TYPE: Biennial, seed or young plant
COLOUR: Purple
PLANTING TIME: Autumn for flowers the following year
FLOWERING TIME: Summer
HEIGHT: 120cm/48in
SOIL: Acid, moist

Primrose *(Primula vulgaris)*
The primrose has suffered greatly in the wild from being overpicked, but makes an excellent garden plant. It prefers a moist, partially shaded spot under trees or hedges.

TYPE: Perennial, seed or young plant
COLOUR: Yellow
PLANTING TIME: Early spring
FLOWERING TIME: Spring
HEIGHT: 20cm/8in
SOIL: Moist

Peter McHoy

other undesirable plants to grow in a tiny patch out of sight. Although they are not particularly attractive to us, butterflies and other wildlife love them. A space behind a shed or garage is ideal.

If you are lucky enough to have taken over a new house with a completely bare plot, you can plan the whole garden for wild flowers. Most people, however, decide to introduce them gradually, perhaps making a single wild flower bed or turning the lawn into a meadow. If you have some trees and shrubs then you might want to create a mini-woodland, with carpets of bluebells and shade-loving plants. Even a small pond can have some wild plants in and around it, or better still you might create a marshy area nearby to grow damp-loving plants like purple loosestrife and marsh marigold. As well as increasing the range of plants you can grow, a marshland makes a great home for frogs and toads.

Making a selection
Whatever size your garden, even if you are gardening on a balcony or patio, there are wild flowers to suit you. The main thing to remember is that you do not have to give the whole garden over to wild flowers straight away (although once you get 'hooked' it's easy to get carried away!). Pick and choose the plants and the habitats that suit your circumstances.

First look at the garden to assess the 'habitats' you already have. A large tree is a good starting point, as you can plant a selection of shade-loving bulbs like snowdrops and bluebells around the base.

Bluebells are a woodland plant and are at home in the dappled shade of trees and larger shrubs (left). If you can give them enough space and the right growing conditions, they will spread themselves happily. Bluebell seeds are available, and are usually sold as Hyacinthoides non-scripta, but are also sometimes known as Endymion non-scriptus.

To some people, the red dead nettles growing among these primulas in a cool but sunny border (right) are weeds. But a weed is only a plant growing in the wrong place, and if you like a native plant it deserves a place in your flower garden. You may sometimes find you need to thin these plants quite ruthlessly though, as they can be rampant growers if they are made welcome.

Photos Horticultural

You could also put in groups of primroses and sweet violets followed by red campion for the summer. A wet spot or the margins of a pond can be turned into a mini-wetland. This is the place to grow moisture-loving plants like the delicate cuckoo flower, yellow flag iris, meadowsweet and ragged robin. Even the pond itself can have native plants, and planting some curled pondweed or spiked water milfoil which grow under water will help to keep the water clean and clear.

Other wild flowers prefer a

PROJECT
COLLECT YOUR OWN SEEDS

Once you have started growing a few wild flowers in the garden, it is easy and economical to collect your own seed to grow into more plants or to pass on to other gardening friends.

● Wait until the seed pods are ripe. This will vary from plant to plant but is usually when the pods have turned from green to brown.
● Snip off the seed pods with scissors or small secateurs and place them inside a paper bag. Shake the bag until all the seed has been released.
● Lay the contents of the bag on a tray and pick out any bits of stem or plant debris. Leave the seed to dry in the sun or in a warm spot indoors. Store the dry seed in paper envelopes or in clean, sealed jars – spice jars are ideal.

Remember to collect only one type of seed at a time and mark the envelopes and jars clearly to avoid mixing up different species.

No specialist equipment is required for you to begin collecting seeds. Dried seed can be kept in airtight storage jars or an envelope until it is needed. Jars should be clearly labelled (right) as many smaller seeds look very much alike.

Marshall Cavendish

Harry Smith Collection

sunny spot and a soil that has been turned over and are best grown in a separate flower bed. Poppies, cornflowers, corncockles and corn marigolds are annuals which flower for only one year. Choose a sunny position in the garden and they will provide you with beautiful cut flowers all summer long. It is also easy to add perennial wild flowers to an existing herbaceous border. Plants like meadow cranes-bill, harebell and musk mallow will flower year after year and bring a host of bees and butterflies to your cottage garden border.

Meadow flowers

You might want to try making a wild flower meadow instead of a smooth lawn. If you have an area of bare earth, you can sow a new flowering lawn with meadow mixture. These seed mixtures, available from some garden centres or by mail order from specialist seedsmen, have the right balance of grasses and low-growing wild flowers and are best sown in the autumn. If you already have an established lawn, let it grow then weed out some of the undesirables such as thistles and dock and put cowslips, ox-eye daisies and lady's bedstraw in their place.

Maintaining a wild flower lawn is quite straightforward; continue to mow it, but to a

height of 5-7cm/2-3in rather than the usual 2.5cm/1in. The only exception is from late spring to mid-summer, the main flowering period, when you need to leave the grass uncut to allow the flowers to produce and spread their seeds.

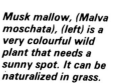

Insight Picture Library

Wild flowers are perfect for a cottage garden border (above), and they can all be grown from seed. Little pockets of soil in wall crevices will encourage ferns and other plants to make a home there.

N.I. Garwood/NHPA

Plants naturally grow best in their favourite type of habitat. A boggy area (above) provides the perfect setting for damp-garden plants. If you have a pond, growing plants in the water will help to keep the water clear, as well as adding to the 'wild' look. There is a wide range of moisture-loving plants available in special garden centres. This sort of garden can be made on a very small scale in a damp, shady corner.

Musk mallow, (Malva moschata), (left) is a very colourful wild plant that needs a sunny spot. It can be naturalized in grass.

Growing wild flowers from seed can be time consuming but is not difficult. Annual seeds such as poppies and cornflowers can be sown straight out in the garden in the spring and will flower the same summer.

A wild flower garden is not a neglected garden and will need some regular maintenance, particularly if it is not to become overgrown. Watering is not usually necessary, except for plants grown in containers which dry out quickly in the summer. Likewise, feeding is unnecessary and most wild species prefer no added fertilizer.

The most important task is to deadhead some of the more invasive plants. Simply cut off the heads after they have flowered to stop the seeds being

PRESSING WILD FLOWERS

To prolong the beauty of your wild flowers, you can dry and press them to make pictures or greetings cards. The delicate colours and shapes can be perfectly preserved either as whole flowers or as individual petals. The secret of successful pressing is to cut the flowers on a dry day and to press them immediately, before the colours begin to fade.

You can buy a simple wooden flower press from a craft shop or you can put the flowers between sheets of newspaper or blotting paper weighted down under heavy books. Make sure that the flowers are laid out absolutely flat in one single layer. Leave in a dry room with a minimum temperature of 10°C (50°F) for 3-4 weeks.

BRIGHT IDEAS

Cowslips (below) are a favourite country plant which used to grow wild in huge numbers. Now they are much less common. Like so many wild flowers, the cowslip is a medicinal plant.

spread around. If your aim is to create a cottage garden, this is less important, as a few flowers which have seeded themselves in unexpected places add to the natural, informal effect.

Whatever you do, do not dig up plants you see in hedgerows or in wild places. Apart from the fact that many of the plants are protected by law, they need all the help they can get to survive. Buy your wild flowers as seeds, bulbs or plants from a reputable nursery, then you can be sure you are helping to increase the species. If you are impatient to see the finished result, the quickest way is to buy small, partly-grown plantlets in spring or summer, which can be planted in a pot or straight into the garden when you get them home. Buy bulbs in the autumn and plant in exactly the same way as daffodils or crocus bulbs.

Michael Leach/NHPA

Budget Gardens

Watching the pennies? Sensible money-saving tips can help you hang onto your cash without sacrificing results in any area of the garden.

Emma Lee/Life File

With a little planning and effort, your borders can be an exciting mix of interesting plants and colours. All these plants (above) could have been bought ready-grown from a garden centre. At much less expense, however, you can grow them yourself from seed or tubers or propagate them from cuttings taken from the gardens of friends and relatives. There is real satisfaction in looking at a lovely border of plants that you have nurtured from scratch.

Gardening doesn't have to be an expensive hobby. With judicious recycling, some good gardening friends, a bit of patience and basic DIY skills, you can have a garden quite as good as your neighbours' for a fraction of the price.

Growing your own plants from seed or cuttings saves money and is fun. But don't economize on proper sowing and cuttings compost – this is one thing you cannot do without. Garden soil, even if sterilized, is not a good enough propagating medium.

Take cuttings

Get cuttings from friends; not just of pot plants, geraniums and fuchsias, but of shrubs, roses and hedging plants as well. A book on propagation will tell you what sort of cuttings to take from which plants and when to take them for best results. Take cuttings of your own plants too.

Strike cuttings of half hardy perennials in pots in late summer and keep them on a window-sill indoors for the winter. This works for verbena, pelargonium, fuchsia, penstemon and many others and is much cheaper than buying new plants every spring. When you buy a new plant – for indoors or out – take cuttings and give some to a friend. That way, if your plant dies you always know where to go for a free replacement!

Rooted pelargonium cuttings (above) will form a lovely summer display. Take 8cm/ 3in tip cuttings for standards in midsummer and for large bush types in early autumn. Overwinter in a light, frost- free place.

Propagate stinking iris (Iris foetidissima) from its seeds (right) or by dividing its rhizomes.

Collect ripe seeds from your hellebores (below right) during the summer.

Andrew Lawson

RECYCLING TIPS

- Compost all kitchen and garden waste to make your own free soil improver.
- When enlarging flower beds, strip off and stack the turves for loam to make your own potting composts.
- Sterilize ingredients (except fertilizer) for potting composts in roasting bags in an oven set at the lowest temperature (50°C/122°F) for 1½ hours. Sterilize ingredients separately before mixing the compost, then spread them out in trays to 'breathe' for a few days before use.
- Buy second-hand garden tools from junk shops, jumble sales or car boot sales. You can get broken tools cheaply re-handled at some tool shops, or you can buy the handles and do it yourself.
- Swap gardening magazines with a friend.
- Make tree ties from lengths of hosepipe with wire threaded through.
- Re-use plastic vending machine cups as pots (make a hole in the base with a hot skewer).
- Re-use fruit punnets as seed trays; transparent plastic supermarket meat/veg trays make good propagator lids.
- Save old tights to hang up shallots and onions to store for winter.
- Save fruit tree prunings to use as pea sticks next year.
- Instead of buying new plant labels each year, clean the old ones with wire wool and washing up liquid and re-use them.

Photos Horticultural

Work out seed orders with friends. Then you can share a packet of cabbage seeds, for instance, instead of buying a packet each. Or get several friends to each grow a few packets of seed, and share the plants with the whole group. And if buying a lot of seed, look out for special collections (particularly of vegetable seeds) which are sometimes offered in seed catalogues.

Saving seed

When sowing, do not use the entire packet of seed at once – you'll end up with far more plants than you need. Instead, sow a small pinch and use the rest for successional sowings, or save it for next year.

If you feel adventurous, try saving seed from your own plants. Seeds worth saving are those of trees and shrubs, peas, beans, bulbs and flowers other than F1 hybrid varieties. Allow the pods to dry right out on the plant; gather fruits and berries when they are over-ripe and fall naturally from the plant. Remove seed from pods, and wash the flesh from seeds of fruit or berries.

Sow or swap tree and shrub seed immediately after collection for best results. Store that of annuals and vegetables in an airtight container, ready for sowing the next spring.

Join a society

A good local gardening club is well worth the membership fee. Clubs often negotiate a discount for their members at local garden centres. And by ordering as a group, you can get substantial discounts on seeds and bulbs from some of the large companies.

Some clubs even have their own trading hut to sell fertilizers and other gardening items at special rates. Many own and lend out the sort of equipment you only use once in a while, like fertilizer spreaders or powered lawn rakers. Club 'bring and buy' sales are a cheap source of plants, and a good way of disposing of your surplus stock.

Some national societies can also be good value. The Royal Horticultural Society, Alpine Garden Society and Hardy Plant Society all run seed dis-

Peter McHoy

PROJECT   MAKE YOUR OWN 'STONE'

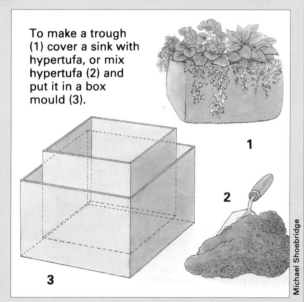

To make a trough (1) cover a sink with hypertufa, or mix hypertufa (2) and put it in a box mould (3).

1

2

3

Michael Shoebridge

Make your own garden containers, ornaments and even fake rock from hypertufa. Simply mix together equal parts of peat, sharp sand and cement with enough water to make it sticky.

To make fake rocks, urns, sculptures or other ornaments cover a shape made from scrunched up wire netting with hypertufa. Or use it to give a fake stone finish to an old glazed sink (spread an outdoor adhesive over the glaze first to give it something to grip to).

You can make your own containers by using two cardboard boxes, one slightly smaller than the other. Place a 4cm/1½in layer of mixture in the base of the bigger box and stand the second inside it, leaving a gap all round the edges. Fill this with more of the mixture. When the mixture is thoroughly set (after several weeks) tear the cardboard away.

Photos Horticultural

Spring is the time to sow hardy annual seeds in the garden (above). Collect the ripe seed from your plants in autumn and store it in an airtight container over the winter.

Photos Horticultural

There is no need to buy a lot of different fertilizers for your garden plants. Manufacturers, of course, are in the business of selling as many different products as they can. All you actually need are two liquid or soluble fertilizers – one general purpose and one high in potash – and a good dry fertilizer, such as Growmore (above right).

The decision to buy power tools will depend on your budget and how much time and energy you have to spend in the garden. An electric lawn-raker (left) will make short work of removing moss and dead grass from your lawn and is probably worth the investment and running costs if you have a large area of grass. The alternatives are to spend longer using an inexpensive lawn rake or to borrow or hire a machine when you need one.

BONE MEAL

GROWMORE

FISH, BLOOD AND BONE

tribution schemes which allow members to draw a number of packets of free seed as a 'perk' of membership.

Buying garden products

Choose a few general purpose products you can use all round the garden, instead of lots of specialized ones. A versatile fertilizer like Growmore or Blood, Fish and Bone can be used on lawns, flowers and vegetables, both as a pre-planting feed and during the growing season.

Two liquid or soluble feeds – one general purpose and the other high in potash (tomato feed) – are all you need for house and greenhouse plants, tubs and hanging baskets.

Do not buy pesticides and fungicides unless you need them. For small infestations, just wipe mildew or greenfly away with a damp cloth. If you do need chemicals, trigger packs can be the best value in small gardens as you do not need to buy a sprayer, and

nothing goes to waste – you just spray what you need. In a larger garden, it is cheaper to buy a concentrate and dilute it ready for use.

You should be able to manage without weedkillers entirely. Hand weeding and hoeing are cheaper and environmentally safer. And by making your own compost, you can be sure of a regular free supply of material for soil improvement and mulching.

If you also collect dead leaves to make leafmould and stack turves for loam, you can even make your own potting mixtures. A good all-purpose recipe is equal parts of sterilized loam, sharp sand and leafmould or cocopeat. Add a slow-release fertilizer, following the maker's instructions, and mix everything well and use it when fresh.

Buying tools

Avoid gadgets; stick to a few good quality basic tools – a spade, fork, hand trowel and

hoe. Electric mowers are a good buy for small lawns. They are cheaper initially and do not need expensive servicing like petrol mowers.

When you have all the tools and equipment you need, look after them properly to get the maximum working life. Clean and dry tools after use, and paint the blades or prongs with oil to prevent rusting (old sump oil from the car is ideal).

Clean dead grass out from under the mower after use, and oil hedge trimmers and shears. Finally, keep the garden shed locked – thefts of garden equipment are common, and may not be covered by your household insurance.

HANDY HINTS

● Watch out for end of season sales at nurseries and garden centres.
● Grow your own garden canes by planting tall species of bamboo (if you have space), or the ornamental sugar cane *Miscanthus* which has bamboo-like stems. Cut stems after two years when they are hard.

Michael Shoebridge

● Treat bamboo canes, wooden posts and fence panels, timber greenhouse frames and hardwood garden furniture with timber preservative every year to prolong their life.
● Bring cushions from garden seats indoors when not in use to prevent fading in sunlight, and store in a dry place in winter to prevent them mildewing.
● Paint handles of small tools like trowels and secateurs orange so they don't get lost if you put them down in the garden.

Index

Page numbers in *italic* refer to illustrations

A

acacia, false 37, 38
Acanthus 37
achillea 29
    A. filipendula 8, 81
    A. millefolium 8
Agapanthus (African lily) 35
ageratum 43
Ailanthus 37
air layering 32, 33
alpines 9, 27, 47
alyssum 14, *79*
Amaranthus caudatus 7
anaphalis 35
anchusa 37
    A. azurea 8
anemone, Japanese 37
annuals 23, 48
    sowing outdoors 7, 8
Antirrhinum 43
    A. majus 81
Argemone mexicana 60
artemisia *79*
    A. abrotanum 81
aruncus 34, 36
aster 14
    A. novi belgii 'Eckingale
       White' *36*
astilbe 36
avens 8, 35
azalea *79*, 81

B

baby's breath 8
basal cuttings 27, 29
bear's breeches 37
bedding plants 23, 53
    cuttings 27
    greenhouse cultivation 43
    sowing 11, 14
    transplanting 25
beebalm 81
beech 30
begonia *12*, 13
    B. semperflorens 43
bellflower 35
Bellis perennis 6
berberis 53
bergamot 35
biennials 24
    sowing outdoors 6, 9
blackberries 31, *31*

black-eyed Susan 7, 9
blanket flower 8, *8*
bluebell 86
broom 9
busy Lizzie 14, *27*
buttercup *85*

C

calabrese 22
Calendula officinalis 7, 81
camellia 30
camomile *79*, 80, 81
Campanula medium 6
    C. rotundifolia 85
campion, pink *85*
    red 87
candytuft 7
canes, growing your own 93
canna 53
Canterbury bell 6, 24, 57
caragana 9
carnations 81
    layering 32-3
Catalpa 37
Catananche caerulea 8
Centaurea cyanus 7, 86
Chaenomeles 37, *38*
Cheiranthus x *allionii* 6
chemicals 93
cherry 37
cherry pie 81
Chimonanthus praecox 81
chrysanthemum *26*, 29, 35,
    44-9, *79*, 81, 82
    C. carinatum 7, 46, 48
       'Court Jesters' 46, *49*
    C. coccineum 47
    C. frutescens 45, 46, 49
       'Jamaica Primrose' *47*
    C. hosmariense 47, *47*
       Korean *45*, 46
    C. maximum 8, 46, 47
       'Phyllis Smith' *48*
    C. parthenium 46, *47*, 48
    pompon 45-6
       'Bronze Fairie' *48*
    C. rubellum 46-7, *46*
    spray 45-6
       'Pennine Gambol' *45*
    C. weyrichii 48
       'Yvonne Arnaud' *49*
Cineraria maritima 14, 53, 57
cinquefoil 35
cistus 29
Clarkia elegans 7, 62-3
    C. pulchella 7

clematis 33
    C. montana 81
clethra *79*
clianthus 9
climbers 27
    serpentine layering *33*
cloche 25
    plastic bottle *13*, 15
clubs 92
Codiaeum variegatum 33
cold frame 19-20, 25, 43
    building 20
columbine 85
composts 93
coneflower 35
conifers 29
containers 52, 57, 72, 73, 81
Convallaria majalis 81
Convolvulus tricolor 7
Coreopsis grandiflora 8
corncockle 88
cornflower 7, *63*, *84*, 86, 88, 89
Cornus alba 29
cotinus 53
cotoneaster 53
cowslip 85, 88, *89*
cranesbill 35, 37, 65-6
    bloody *67*, 69
    meadow *68*, 69, 88
Crataegus 81
Crocus chrysanthus 81
    C. sativus 81
croton 33
cuckoo flower 87
cupid's dart 8
currant 29
cut flowers 47, 53, 57, 59, *77*,
    80, 82
cuttings 90, *91*
    heel 25, 27, 29
    root 34, 37, 38
    stem 26-9
    transplanting 25
cyclamen *17*
cypress 27, 29

D

daffodils *85*
dahlia *26*, 29, 36, 50-3
    ball, 'Wootton Cupid' *51*
    cactus-flowered *51*
       'Doris Day' *53*
    collerette, 'La Cierva' *51*
    decorative, 'Master Robert'
       50
    dwarf, 'Coltness Hybrids' *52*

daisy 6, *84*, 85
    Livingstone 14
    ox-eye *85*, 88
    Shasta 8, 35, 46, 47
dame's violet 81, *84*
damping off 18
daphne *79*
    D. mezereum 81
day lily 35, *35*, *79*, 81
delphinium 8, *26*, 29, 53, 57,
    70-3
    'Butterball' 73, *73*
    D. consolida 7
    dwarf 70
    'Gordon Forsyth' *71*, 73
    'Lamartine' 73, *73*
    'Langdon's Royal Flush' 72,
       73
    'Lord Butler' *73*
    'Olive Poppleton' *72*, 73
Dendranthema 'Clara Curtis' *46*
    'Raquel' *45*
deutzia 29
Dianthus 68, 81
    D. barbatus 6, *6*
    D. carophyllus 'Cherry Ripe'
       80
Dieffenbachia 33
Digitalis x *mertonensis* 56
    D. purpurea 6, 86
disbudding 45, 49, 52
diseases 45, 51, 55, 59, 66, 71
division 34-7
dogwood 29
dried flowers 59, *62*, 74, *76*
dumb cane 33

E

Echinops ritro 8
elaeagnus 30
    E. pungens 81
Erodium 37
Eryngium 37
Eschscholzia californica 7, 60
euonymus 53
evergreens 29

F

feather grass *62*
fertilizer 93
feverfew *47*, 48
fibrous-rooted plants 35
Ficus (fig) *32*, 33
flax, scarlet 7, *7*
fleabane 35

forget-me-not 6
forsythia 29, 31, 57
foxglove 6, *56*, 57, 86
foxglove tree 37
fragrance 57, 78-83
 garden plan *79*
frost 19
fuchsia 27, 29, 53, 90

G

Gaillardia aristata 8, *8*
Galanthus 81
gardener's garters 63
geranium 27, 29, 37, 65-9, 90
 G. cinereum 67
  'Ballerina' 67, *69*
  subcaulescens 67
 G. clarkei 69
 G. dalmaticum 67
 G. endressii 'Wargrave Pink'
  67, 69
 G. ibericum 38
 'Johnson's Blue' *67*, 69
 G. macrorrhizum 68, 69
 G. nodosum 66
 G. phaeum 66-7, *66*
 G. pratense 69
  'Flore Pleno' *68*
  'Kashmir White' *69*
 G. psilostemon 65, 69
 G. pylzowianum 67
 G. sanguineum 67, 69
 G. s. lancastrense 67, *67*
 G. sylvaticum 'Mayflower' 67
 G. wallichianum 'Buxton's
  Blue' *66*, 67
Geum chiloense 8
gardener's garters 63
goat's beard 36
grape hyacinth 80, 81
greenhouse 25, 40-3
ground-cover *68*, 69
growing on 18
Gypsophila elegans 7
 G. paniculata 8

H

Hamamelis 30
hanging baskets 57, 81
hardening off 18, 19
hardwood cuttings 25, 29
hardy annuals, sowing 7, 8
hardy herbaceous perennials,
 sowing 8, 9
harebell *85*, 88
hawthorn 81
heartsease *84*
heather 29
Hedera helix 'Glacier' *82*
hedge, from cuttings 27, 90
heel cuttings 25, 27, 29
helenium *74*
Helianthus annuus see
 sunflower hellebore *91*
Hemerocallis 35, *35*, 81
herbs 27

Hesperis matronalis 8
holly 30
hollygrape 81, *81*
hollyhock 57
honesty 6
honeysuckle 33, 57, 80
hosta 34, 36
houseplants, layering 33
Hyacinthoides non-scripta 86

I

Iberis umbellata 7
Ilex 30
Indian bean tree 37
indoor growing
 pricking out 15, 16-19
 sowing 11-15
iris 62
 bearded 36, *39*, 82
 I. foetidissima 91
 I. reticulata 81
 root division *36*
 I. sibirica 37
 yellow flag 87
ivy 73, *82*

J

Jasminum (jasmine) 33, 80
 J. officinale 81

K

Kniphofia 35
Kochia childsii 14
 K. tricophylla 14

L

lady's bedstraw 88
lady's mantle 35
larkspur 7, 18, 70, 73
 'Dwarf Hyacinth Mixed' *71*
Lathyrus odoratus see
 sweet pea
Lavandula (lavender) *79*, 81, 82
 cuttings *28*
 L. spica 68
Lavatera olbia 'Rosea' *63*
layering 30-3
Leucojum vernum 81
lilac 38, *79*, 81
 heel cuttings *25*
lily, regal *79*, 81, 82
lily-of-the-valley 81
Limnanthus douglasii 7
Linum grandiflorum 7
 'Rubrum' *7*
Lippia citriodora 81
lobelia 14, 16, 43, 73
loganberry 31
Lonicera 33
 L. japonica 'Aureoreticulata'
  81
loosestrife, purple 86
love-in-a-mist 7
love-lies-bleeding 7

Lunaria annua 6
lupin 12, *12*
 tree *79*

M

Macleaya 60
magnolia 30, 81
Mahonia lomariifolia 81
Malcolmia maritima 7
Malva (mallow) 14
 M. moschata (musk m.) *88*
 tree *63*
marguerite *47*, 49
marigold 43
 African 14
 corn 88
 French 14
 marsh 86
 pot 7, 12, 18, 81, 82
Matthiola bicornis 7
mayweed *63*
meadow, wild flower 88
meadowsweet 87
Meconopsis betonicifolia 60
 M. cambrica 60
mezereon 81
Michaelmas daisy 34, 35, *36*, *39*
mignonette 7, *49*, *79*
mint 36
mock orange *79*, *80*, 81
Monarda didyma 81
money-saving tips 90-3
morning glory 9
mourning widow *66*, 67
mullein 37, 57, *84*
Muscari armeniacum 81
Myosotis 6

N

Narcissus 85
nemesia 14
nicotiana 14, 43, *49*
Nigella damascena 7

O

Osmanthus delavayi 81
 O. heterophyllis 81
outdoor
 sowing 6-10, 18
 transplanting 24-5
oxalis 57

P

pansy 14, *17*
Papaver 37
 P. alpinum 60, 62, *62*
 P. commutatum 61
  'Lady Bird' *60*, 61, 62
 P. nudicaule 60-1, 62
  'Summer Breeze' *59*
 P. orientale 8, 62
 P. rhoeas 7, 61-2, *63*, 86
  'Diana' *58*
  'Shirley Single

Mixed' *58*
 P. somniferum 62, *62*
  'Pink Chiffon' *61*
 see also poppy
Paulownia 37
pearl everlasting 35
pelargonium 29, 65, 90, *91*
penny royal 81
penstemon 90
peony 36, *79*, 82
perennials 24
 cuttings 27
 root propagation 34, 38
 sowing outdoors 8, 9
pests 45, 51, 55, 59, 66, 71, 93
petunia 14, *21*, 43
Phalaris arundinacea 'Picta' 63
philadelphus 29, *80*
 P. coronarius 81
philodendron 33
phlox 35, 37, *79*
 P. paniculata 81
pieris 30
pinks *79*, 81
 clove *80*
planthouses 40, *41*
planting out 20, *21*
plugs 23
poached egg plant 7
poisonous plants 63
polyanthus 24
polypropylene fleece 25
ponds 86, 87
poppy 18, 58-63, *84*, 88, 89
 alpine 60, 62, *62*
 Californian 7, 60
 field 7, 58, *58*, 61-3, *63*, 86
 Himalayan blue 60
 Iceland 59, *59*, 60-3, *61*
 opium 60, *61*, 62-3, *62*, *63*
 oriental 8, 37, 58-9, *58*, 61-3
 plume 60
 prickly 60
 tree 37, 60
 Welsh 60, *84*
pot pourri 81-2
potentilla 29
potting up 24
pressing wild flowers 89
pricking out 15, 16-20, 21-3
Primula (primrose) 35, 85, 87
 evening 81
 P. denticulata 37
 P. vulgaris 86
propagators *14-15*
Prunus 38
pyrethrum 35
 P. roseum 47, *47*

Q

quince, flowering 37

R

ragged robin 87
raised beds 81, *82*
recycling 91

red hot poker 35
Reseda odorata 7
rhizomes 36
rhododendron 30, *31*, 81
Rhus 37, 53
Ricinus communis 14
Robinia 37, 38
rockery 58, 67-9
rocket, sweet 8
Romneya 37, 60
root propagation 34-8
    cuttings 34, 37, 38
rooting powder 28
Rosa (rose) 57, 63, *78-9*, 80,
    82, 90
    'Aloha' *69*
    cuttings 25, 27, 29
rubber plant 33
Rubus 37
rudbeckia 14
    'Goldsturm' *34*, 35
    R. hirta 7, 9

S

salvia 14, 29, 81
saxifrage 35, *57*
screens 77, *77*
sea holly 37
seedlings 15, *43*
    planting 16-20
    pricking out 15, 16-20, 21-3
    transplanting 21-5
seeds
    collecting 87, *91*, 92
    encouraging *7*, 9, 56

sowing 6-10, 11-15, 18, 89, *92*
    storing 90
semi-ripe cuttings *26*, 29
Senecio cineraria see
    Cineraria maritima
serpentine layering *33*
shrubs 53, 57
    cuttings *25*, 27, 90
    layering 30-1
    sowing outdoors 9
    transplanting 25
silver foliage 68
southernwood 81
snapdragon 79, 81
snowberry 38
snowdrop 80, 81, 86
snowflake 81
societies 92
softwood cuttings 25, *26*, 27, 29
Solomon's seal 36
staging, greenhouse 42, *42*
staking dahlias 52-3, *52*
stem cuttings 26-9
Stipa pennata 62
stock, night-scented 7, *80*, 81
    Virginian 7
stone, making 92
stork's bill 37
strawberry, layering *30*, 33
suckers 37-8
sumach 37
summersweet *79*
sunflower 7, 74-7
    'Autumn Beauty' *75*, 76
    'Giant Single' 75, *75*, 76
    'Russian Giant' 75, 76

'Sunburst Mixed' *75*, 76
'Teddy Bear' 76, *76*
supports 52-3, *52*, 56, 70
sweet pea 7, *7*, 9, 12, *12*, *17*,
    54-7, 82
    'Air Warden' *55*
    dwarf 55, *55*, 56-7
sweet William 6, *6*, 57
Symphoricarpos 37
Syringa 38, 81

T

tagetes 14
Tanacetum haradjanii 68
thistle, globe 8
thuja *27*
thyme *79*, 81
tip cuttings 29
tip layering 31-2, *31*
tobacco plant *79*, 81, *82*
tomato 22, 43
tools 93
transplanting 21-5
tree of heaven 37
trees
    cuttings *25*
    layering 30
    sowing outdoors 9
    transplanting 25

V

vegetables, transplanting 24-5
Verbascum 37
verbena 14, 90

lemon *80*, 81
viburnum *79*
    V. farreri 81
vines 33
violet *79*, 87

W

wallflower 24, 82
    Siberian 6
weigela 29
wet areas 86, 87, *88*
wild flowers 8, *58*, 60, *63*, 84-9
wildlife garden 74, 76, 85-6
willow 27, 29
windbreaks 77, *77*
window boxes 81
wintersweet 81
wisteria 33
witch hazel 30
woodruff, sweet *79*

Y

yarrow 8, 35, 81
yew 27

Z

zinnia 14, 43

Photographic Credits

ANDREW LAWSON *17, 23, 24, 55, 66, 68, 91*
COLLECTIONS *9, 22, 25, 36, 37, 56*; DAVID SQUIRE *39*
DEREK GOULD *7, 52, 67, 76, 80*
ERIC CRICHTON *8, 22, 30, 32, 36, 46, 47, 49, 56, 57, 69, 73, 75, 85*; EWA *11*
GARDEN PICTURE LIBRARY *51, 57, 60, 74, 75, 77, 82*; GILLIAN BECKETT *25, 67, 69, 70*
HARRY SMITH COLLECTION *7, 9, 19, 20, 23, 38, 47, 48, 49, 50, 56, 58, 59, 60, 61, 65, 71, 72, 73, 75, 82, 84, 88*
INSIGHT PICTURE LIBRARY *62, 71, 72, 76, 82, 88*; LIFE FILE *90*
MARSHALL CAVENDISH *18, 26, 27, 28, 29, 31, 37, 38, 52, 53, 55, 72, 78, 80, 87*
NATURE PHOTOGRAPHS *63*; NHPA *85, 88, 89*; PAT BRINDLEY *62, 91*
PETER MCHOY *10, 17, 19, 24, 33, 35, 43, 48, 76, 83, 86, 92*
PHOTOS HORTICULTURAL *6, 12, 17, 18, 22, 27, 34, 35, 44, 45, 46, 47, 50, 51, 53, 55, 58, 64, 66, 80, 81, 87, 90, 91, 92, 93*
RAY DUNS *11*; S & O MATHEWS *51, 54, 68, 78*
SUN GREENHOUSES, TAMWORTH *40, 41, 42*; TANIA MIDGLEY *21, 63*